DEVELOPING RESEARCH SKILLS

INDEPENDENT RESEARCH PROJECTS ON ANIMALS AND PLANTS

WRITTEN AND ILLUSTRATED BY

JANET CAUDILL BANKS, MA

DEVELOPING RESEARCH SKILLS

INDEPENDENT RESEARCH PROJECTS ON ANIMALS AND PLANTS

By Janet Caudill Banks, MA

First Edition, August, 1992

Revised Edition, September, 1993

Revised Edition, August, 1995

Copyright © CATS Publications
(Creative Activities and Teaching Strategies)
8633 233rd Place S.W.
Edmonds, WA 98026
(425) 776-0344

ISBN 1-886753-00-8

CURRICULUM BOOKS

Creating and Assessing Performance-Based Curriculum Projects (Grades K-8) ISBN 1-886753-19-9
A teacher's guide to project-based learning and performance assessment. Includes strategies for planning and writing thematic curriculum projects that contain authentic assessment tools for guiding and judging student performance. Projects are to be based on essential learnings standards, and need to provide for assessment of concepts, skills, learner characteristics, and learning processes students go through as they complete projects.

Creating the Multi-Age Classroom (Grades 1-8) ISBN 1-886753-03-2
A guidebook for operating a multi-age classroom, outlining changes needed in organization, curriculum, instructional strategies, assessment and evaluation. Considerations for starting a program, techniques for classroom management, and projects for developing higher-level thinking skills are also included, along with ways to improve questioning strategies, ideas for teaching math and literature, and forms for student record keeping.

Creative Projects for Independent Learners (Grades 3-8) ISBN 1-886753-02-4
Activities involve students with literature, comprehension skills, writing, spelling, research skills, and dictionary studies, while developing higher-level thinking skills. Projects are designed for individuals and small groups and help students to become self-directed learners.

Enhancing Research Skills (Intermediate and Middle School) ISBN 1-886753-01-6
Independent research activities on the Civil War. Students will learn about the war as they locate information, fill in an outline, take notes, organize material, write a rough draft, revise, edit, proofread, and complete a finished report. Also included are thematic research projects, using inquiries, which will promote higher-level thinking skills, while providing additional information for student reports.

Essential Learnings of Mathematics (Grades 3-6) ISBN 1-886753-04-0
An organizational framework for developing concepts and procedures throughout the strands of mathematics, following state and national standards. Includes rationale for math reform, student objectives and vocabulary, techniques for classroom management, explorations and investigations from real-life experiences, strategies for teaching problem solving, and suggestions for performance assessment.

LANGUAGE GAMES (Grades 3-8)
Card games stressing language and dictionary skills, designed for partners or small groups and perfect for learning centers. Cards are printed on cardstock and need to be cut apart before playing.

Idiom Games   "Define It or Fake It" and "Idiom's Delight"

Multiple Meaning Games   "Focus on the Meaning" and "What Could It Possibly Be?"

Guide Word Games   "Quick on the Draw" and "Guide Word Scramble"

Synonym, Antonym, Homonym Games   "Rocket Match Game" and "Synonym, Antonym Antics"

Dictionary Research Board Games   "What's My 'Cat'egory?" and "Guess Our Size"

Context Clue Games   "Consider the Context" and "Sensible Nonsense"

GEOGRAPHY GAMES (Ages 10 to adult)
Card games using information about states and countries, which players read aloud to opponents as sets of clues. Opponents then try to determine which state or country is being described. On cardstock, these games are ready to play, in class, at home, and when traveling.

United States Geography-Geology Game   "State Solutions" (includes all 50 states)

World Geography Game   "Country Clues" (includes 50 countries)

FOREWORD

Students who work their way through the animal unit will be able to write any research report, as they will understand how to follow an outline, take notes, organize information, edit, revise, proofread, and publish a final copy. Students are able to understand the animal unit as they work their way through it due to the general knowledge of animals they already have. As a result of completing this unit they will have an understanding of how to apply these skills to other topics, make up outlines, take notes in an organized manner, and put together a thoroughly organized final product.

Students who complete the activities in the plant unit will have a chance to experience three different approaches to research: report writing activities following outlines and notetaking, organization and report writing activities using mindmapping and notetaking, and research activities involving experiments and investigations following the action verbs from Bloom's Taxonomy which help to develop higher level thinking.

I have found these units to be very valuable in developing self-directed learners, capable of doing excellent research projects. Skills that your students learn will carry over to other areas of the curriculum and will continue to be useful to them throughout their school careers. What they will learn here will be the same as what they will need at higher education levels. I truly believe that these units can help students to become lifelong learners.

Janet C. Banks

DEDICATION

This book is dedicated to my parents,

Sylvan and Lucille Caudill,

with appreciation for their strong commitment to education.

Both having been dedicated teachers themselves,

they passed on their love of learning

and always gave me support and encouragement

throughout my teaching career.

TABLE OF CONTENTS

v

SECTION ONE

TEACHER REFERENCE GUIDE

ANIMAL UNIT

CONTENTS OF THE ANIMAL RESEARCH UNIT:
CONTRACT PACKET

TEACHER'S GUIDE: ANIMAL UNIT DIRECTIONS

STUDENT CONTRACT FORM

PROGRESS REPORT: ANIMAL UNIT

FINAL REPORT REQUIREMENTS

FINAL REPORT EVALUATION

ANSWER KEY: FOR STUDENT WORK PAGES--ANIMAL UNIT

PLANT UNIT

CONTENTS OF THE PLANT RESEARCH UNIT

TEACHER'S GUIDE: PLANT UNIT DIRECTIONS

ANSWER KEY: FOR STUDENT WORK PAGES--PLANT UNIT

CONTENTS OF THE ANIMAL RESEARCH UNIT: CONTRACT PACKET

Some of the materials in the contract packet are divided into two strands. The lessons in the green strand section are easier than the lessons in the blue strand. Green strand lessons are for students who are just beginning to learn research skills and note taking, while blue strand lessons are for students who have had some experience, and/or are capable of breaking the information down into more subtopics.

1. Page 11 is a student-teacher contract to be signed by the teacher and the student, in which the student agrees to complete the packet. Notes may be recorded from consultations with students as they are working. The contract also includes space for final evaluation comments.

2. Page 12 is a student progress report for the student to use to keep track of due dates and completion of assignments throughout the unit.

3. Page 13 is to be given to the students before they write their final reports. It explains the minimum requirements for student reports, and tells students how much each part of the assignment is worth. Teachers will need to fill in the number of points according to their own discretion. Due dates are to be recorded on this sheet. Students are also told to prepare a 10-15 minute oral report.

4. Page 14 is a final report evaluation sheet for teacher use.

5. Pages 15-16 are answer key pages for the consumable student work pages in the animal unit.

6. Pages 28-36 (Green) and 48-56 (Blue) are student contract booklets, explaining to students what is necessary to complete their contracts for the animal unit. Student contract pages include:
    Goals (what students are expected to learn)
    An outline of activities students will perform
    A list of evidence to use to show completion of the contract
    Resources and materials needed
    Procedures to follow

Contents of the Animal Contract Packet (continued)

7. Pages 31 (Green) and 51 (Blue) explain the resources and materials that will need to be provided for this unit, including library books, films, and filmstrips. ENCYCLOPEDIAS ARE OFF LIMITS! Children need to use library books for this unit so they will learn how to organize information. Students are also directed not to use library materials that already have information separated into the categories they are looking for.

8. Pages 37 (Green) and 57 (Blue) are animal lists for the students to choose from. Common animals are listed so that written information will be available. Animals found on the green list are the most common and easiest to locate. Some of the animals on the blue list are more difficult to locate in library materials. The two strands of projects, for students of different ability levels, will be explained more thoroughly below.

9. Pages 38 (Green) and 58-59 (Blue) are the animal report outlines to be followed. The blue outline is broken down into more subtopics for the more able student to follow.

10. Pages 39, 41 (Green) and 60-61, 63-64 (Blue) are information sheets containing the information needed for organizing and note taking lessons.

11. Pages 40 (Green) and 62 (Blue) are organization sheets explaining how to cut apart notes and reorganize them according to outlines.

12. Pages 42-45 (Green) and 65-69 (Blue) are practice sheets for note writing.

13. Pages 46 (Green) and 70 (Blue) are pages explaining to students how they are to write their final research reports.

14. Pages 72-73 are the worksheets needed by all students for the first assignment, learning to locate information in library books.

15. Pages 74-81 are note taking lessons for all students to complete.

16. Page 82 is a list of note taking hints for all students to follow.

17. Pages 83-84 are practice sheets for all students to learn how to write sentences in plural form.

18. Page 85 includes report writing hints for all students to consider.

Contents of the Animal Contract Packet (continued)

19. Page 86 includes editing, revising, and proofreading hints for all students to follow.

20. Page 87 is a page explaining to all students what needs to be done to finish their animal research reports.

FOR TEACHER INFORMATION:

Organization and Reproduction of Animal Unit Pages

Pages for Directions Only
(copies could just be discussed then posted for student referral, or stapled together into booklets for student use as needed)

Green Strand	Blue Strand
28-36	48-56
37	57
40	62
46	70

Green and Blue Strands
82
85
86
87

For Teacher And Student Use
15-16

Consumable Student Pages
(copies needed by each student to write on, or to use as guides for writing and note taking)

Green Strand	Blue Strand
38	58-59
39	60-61
41	63-64
42-45	65-69

Green and Blue Strands
72-73
74-75
76-77
78-79
80-81
83-84

For Teacher and Student Use
11
12
13
14

TEACHER'S GUIDE: ANIMAL UNIT DIRECTIONS

This unit consists of a student contract packet that can be copied for each student to follow, or several copies can be made available for students to share. Each student should complete the unit lessons independently, but activities should be discussed in cooperative group situations whenever possible. Many library books need to be available for students to examine. Teachers should guide students through these activities, but leave them to think for themselves and/or to work cooperatively with peers.

Some of the lessons may be taught as whole class lessons or small group activities. There are two different strands throughout the unit to help students with varying abilities. Materials labeled "GREEN" are easier than those labeled "BLUE." Teacher discretion should be used as to which strand each student should follow. Students who have had little experience with note taking and outlining should follow the green strand, unless a teacher feels they would be able to handle the more difficult lessons. Students who have had more experience would benefit from completing the blue strand. See the following directions for an explanation of activities:

NOTE: GREEN STRAND MATERIALS ARE FOUND IN SECTION TWO IN THIS BOOK, BLUE STRAND MATERIALS ARE FOUND IN SECTION THREE, AND MATERIALS NEEDED FOR BOTH STRANDS ARE FOUND IN SECTION FOUR.

Pages 28-30 (Green)-Pages 48-50 (Blue)

The goals are listed for the contract, along with a list of the activities that will be completed for the unit. A list of evidence for the students to show that they have fulfilled the contract is included.

Page 31 (Green)-Page 51 (Blue)
A list of resources and materials to be used is given.

Pages 32-36 (Green)-Pages 52-56 (Blue)

The procedures to be followed throughout the unit are described in these pages. Students are told exactly what to do and in what order. They are told which worksheets, information sheets, organization sheets, practice sheets, note taking sheets, and outline sheets, they will need to obtain in order to complete the following lessons:

PROCEDURES

Lesson directions and explanation of the materials needed for the animal unit, as outlined in the student contract.

Lesson 1

A large variety of library books will need to be available for this lesson. Students will be trying to locate different animals, first by title, then by using an index, then by examining a table of contents. They will skim and scan books that do not have an index or a table of contents, if the title suggests the animal will be described somewhere in the book.

Lesson 2

Students will choose an animal from their wild animal lists for this lesson. (Green, p. 37-Blue, p. 57) They are to use Worksheets 1 and 2, pp. 72-73, for writing down the titles and authors of five books that include information on the animal they are looking for. They are to write the page numbers from each book to show where this information is found.

Lesson 3

Using the above mentioned books, students from both strands are to copy sentences from each book, using Worksheets 1 and 2, which they have started in Lesson 2. The purpose of this and the following lessons will be to find and organize information. Information does not need to be written in the students' own words at this point. Students should note the categories on description, home, food, protection, and young, and try to include information on as many of these categories as possible in order to benefit from the next lesson.

Lesson 4

Students should use their animal report outlines, (Green, p. 38-Blue, pp. 58-59) along with Worksheets 1 and 2 for this lesson. They will look at each sentence they have written and determine where it would fit according to the outline. They will then label each sentence according to the directions given.

Lesson 5

Students will use the information gathered and labeled in the first four lessons to write a mini-report, following the order of the outline. They should write five different paragraphs, if possible, even if they only have one sentence to fit a category.

6

Lessons 6 and 7

Students will need the animal report outlines, organization sheets, and information sheets as listed in step 6 of their contracts. The organization sheets tell them to label each statement on the information sheets, then cut them apart and reorganize the sentences according to the outlines. They will then be pasting these strips down on a piece of paper in the order they have chosen.

Chipmunk	Butterfly
Animal Report Outline: Green, Page 38	Animal Report Outline: Blue, Pages 58-59
Information Sheet: Green 1, Page 39	Information Sheets: Blue 1-2, Pages 60-61
Organization Sheet: Green, Page 40	Organization Sheet: Blue, Page 62

Lessons in the blue strand break the topics down further into more subtopics for the students to use while they are organizing their information. The blue strand lessons also include more notes for students to organize than the green strand lessons do, making them more difficult.

NOTE: ALL STUDENTS WILL COMPLETE LESSON 8, WHETHER ON THE GREEN OR THE BLUE STRAND.

Lesson 8

Students are directed to complete Note Taking Sheets 1-8, Pages 74-81.

Note Taking Sheets 1 and 2--Students are asked to underline the key words in sentences on snails, tapirs, snakes, and koalas. These are the words that would be used if they were taking notes on these animals for reports.

Note Taking Sheets 3 and 4--Students are asked to write the key words about jaguars and muskrats, in note form, after each sentence given.

Note Taking Sheets 5 and 6--Students are asked to determine categories for each statement on lions and frogs, as well as writing the information in note form under the correct headings.

Note Taking Sheets 7 and 8--Students are asked to change notes on bobcats and red foxes to sentence form.

Lesson 9

Students are told to read "Note Taking: Hints for Students," page 82.

Lesson 10

Students are directed to locate information on prairie dogs (Green), or spiders (Blue) to complete this lesson, along with the note writing practice pages. They will still need their animal report outlines.

Prairie Dogs	Spiders
Animal Report Outline: Green, Page 38	Animal Report Outline: Blue, Pages 58-59
Information Sheet: Green 2, Page 41	Information Sheets: Blue 3-4, Pages 63-64
Note Writing Practice: Green 1-4, Pages 42-45	Note Writing Practice: Blue 1-5, Pages 65-69

Using the above pages, students are to read information on prairie dogs and/or spiders and label each statement according to their outlines. They are then to transfer this information to their practice sheets, the note writing practice pages, in note form.

NOTE: STUDENTS SHOULD UNDERSTAND AT THIS POINT HOW TO TAKE NOTES IN NOTE FORM AND HOW TO ORGANIZE THEM, ACCORDING TO THEIR OUTLINES. AS THEY CONTINUE WITH THE NEXT LESSON, THEY WILL LEARN TO TAKE THEIR NOTES IN AN ORGANIZED MANNER. WHEN THEIR NOTES ARE COMPLETED, THEY WILL UNDERSTAND HOW TO USE THEM TO WRITE AN ORGANIZED REPORT.

NOTE: ALL STUDENTS WILL COMPLETE THE SAME ASSIGNMENTS FOR LESSONS 11-15.

Lesson 11

All students will need enough note cards to label for each subtopic in their outlines, as well as a bibliography card. They should use two cards for Description, one for each subtopic, then use two for Home, two for Food, two for Protection, and three for Young. Students following the blue strand may wish to label their cards in more detail to make it easier to separate their information later. (See directions in the student contract.)

Lessons 12-13

Students are directed to take notes on an animal of their choice, reading each sentence carefully and determining which note card the information should be written on. They are directed to use note form, and not to write complete sentences. They are also told to keep track of the books and page numbers they are using. They are to try to locate information for each of their note cards. When they have enough information, they are told to go on to lesson 14.

Lesson 14

Students are to read "Report Writing: Hints for Students," page 85. Many suggestions are given to help them to write a better report from their notes.

Lesson 15

Pages 83-84, "Working With Singular and Plural Form," are to be completed. These lessons are to help the students to write their reports in the plural form. They will probably need teacher direction, as these lessons are difficult, but students from both strands should complete these lessons before they try to write their reports. Students have a difficult time keeping their reports written in plural form, and these activities will help them to see that their meaning is not clear when they switch back and forth between singular and plural form, while they are writing.

Teacher's Guide: Animal Unit Directions (continued)

Lesson 16

Pages entitled "How to Write Your Animal Research Report" are to be read and discussed. (Green, page 46-Blue, page 70) Directions are given to explain to the students how to use their notes, follow their outlines, and write their rough draft in an organized manner.

NOTE: ALL STUDENTS WILL COMPLETE THE SAME ASSIGNMENTS FOR LESSONS 17-19.

Lesson 17

Students are directed to edit, revise, and proofread their rough drafts. They are told to read "Editing, Revising, and Proofreading: Hints for Students," page 86, before they begin. They are also asked to have two people, other than their teacher, read their rough draft to help them with corrections. It is wonderful to get parents involved at this stage, if they are willing to do so. Ask the students to have these people sign at the end of the rough draft, after they have read it, so you will know who helped the students with corrections.

Lesson 18

Students are to write their final drafts, and then follow "How to Finish Your Animal Research Report," page 87, which tells them how to finish their reports. Directions are given to include a bibliography, make a cover, and draw or copy pictures for their reports.

Lesson 19

Directions are given to turn in note cards, rough drafts, and final copies of reports.

STUDENT CONTRACT FORM

This agreement is between:

_____and_____
            (Teacher)   (Student)

Grade sought: (or amount to be completed)   Date_____

Consultations:

Date   Comments

Final Evaluation:

Date   Comments

PROGRESS REPORT: ANIMAL UNIT

ASSIGNMENT	Date Due	Date Completed
1. Worksheet One Information Written		
2. Worksheet One Labeled		
3. Mini-report Written		
4. Note Labeling Assignment Completed		
5. Note Taking Lessons 1 and 2 Finished		
6. Note Taking Lessons 3 and 4 Finished		
7. Note Taking Lessons 5 and 6 Finished		
8. Note Taking Lessons 7 and 8 Finished		
9. Note Taking Practice Pages Completed		
10. Final Report--Notes Written		
11. Final Report--Rough Draft Written		
12. Final Report--Rough Draft Corrected		
13. Final Report Written and Turned In		

FINAL REPORT
REQUIREMENTS

Minimum requirement is _____ sentences, average length. This would be an average of _____ sentences for each section of your outline. Some sections will have more and some will have less depending on the nature of your animal.

Reports will be evaluated in the following way:

Points will be given for:

Notes (amount)--the amount of notes taken

Notes (quality of organization)--how well the notes fit the outline topics

Report (rough draft)--completion and correction of rough draft

Report (organization)--how well the report follows the outline topics

Report (mechanics)--spelling, punctuation, appearance, sentence form, paragraphing, etc.

Report (extras)--additions, cover, pictures, drawings, etc.

Oral Report (10-15 minute presentation)--to include the most interesting facts from your report, and the picture of your animal

Each area is worth the following:

Notes (amount)   _____pts.

Notes (quality of organization)   _____pts.

Report (rough draft)   _____pts.

Report (organization)   _____pts.

Report (mechanics)   _____pts.

Report (extras)   _____pts.

Oral report (presentation, content)   _____pts.

13

FINAL REPORT EVALUATION

Notes (amount) _____pts.

Notes (quality of organization) _____pts.

Report (corrected rough draft) _____pts.

Report (organization) _____pts.

Report (mechanics) _____pts.

Report (extras, cover, pictures, etc.) _____pts.

Oral Report (presentation, content) _____pts.

Extra bonus points may have been given for exceptional effort or quality in any of the above areas.

TOTAL POINTS_____   EVALUATION_____

COMMENTS:

ANSWER KEY: STUDENT WORK PAGES

ANIMAL UNIT

Note Writing Practice Pages: Green, pages 42-45 and Blue, pages 65-69

Answers will vary according to the interpretation of students. If notes don't seem to fit the categories chosen, let children explain choices.

Worksheets 1 and 2, pages 72-73

Answers will vary according to the animal chosen and material the student writes in notes.

Note Taking Sheet 1, page 74

Possible Answers (student responses should be similar)

SNAILS

1. Many kinds-live in sea
2. mollusk family
3. foot-help them move
4. largest-live-tropical climate
5. Most-live-spiral-shaped or cone-shaped shells
6. thousands-different kinds
7. soft bodies-without backbones
8. live-ponds, fresh water, rivers, lakes, land

TAPIRS

1. usually timid-try stay away from people
2. heavy, thick set-tiny tails-short legs
3. long nose-upper lips looking like an elephant's trunk
4. eat leaves, twigs
5. mammals-pig-like
6. travel alone or in groups, two or three

Note Taking Sheet 2, page 75

Possible Answers (student responses should be similar)

SNAKES

1. reptiles-crawling animals
2. homes-tree, under bushes, crevices in rocks, under ground
3. live-hot deserts, high mountains, sea, lowlands
4. long, slender-backbones, ribs, scales
5. move-very quickly
6. often shed skins while growing, get new ones
7. eat-frogs, toads, insects, rats, mice, rabbits, birds, fish

15

ANSWER KEY *(continued)*

KOALAS

1. found-continent Australia
2. do not have tails
3. leaves Eucalyptus tree-main food
4. marsupials
5. most time-high eucalyptus tree
6. pouches-pockets of skin-abdomen
7. good climbers

Note Taking Sheet 3, page 76

Possible Answers (student responses should be similar)

JAGUARS

1. hot, tropical areas-from Texas, Mexico through Argentina
2. look like-leopards
3. up to 7 ft. long-200 lbs.
4. big, spotted
5. cat family
6. may cover several hundred miles-travel
7. attack-horses, cattle, even man
8. most-travel alone

Note Taking Sheet 4, page 77

Possible Answers (student responses should be similar)

MUSKRATS

1. look like-large field mice
2. females-2 to 6 babies at a time
3. belong-rodent family-gnawing animals
4. eat-tiny animals found in water-grass-seeds
5. nests-underwater entrances
6. relatives-rat, squirrel, beaver
7. live-in, around-swamps, lakes-many parts of United States

Note Taking Sheet 5, page 78

Notes written will vary, but notes from the following sentences should be included under each category:

LIONS

Description--No's 1,5,6,7,10

Home--No's 2, 9, 14

Food--No's 3,4,8,11,12,13

Note Taking Sheet 6, page 79

Notes written will vary, but notes from the following sentences should be included under each category:

FROGS

Description--No's 2,3,4,7,8

Home--No's 1,6,9,12,13

Food--No's 5,10,11,14

Note Taking Sheets 7 and 8, pages 80-81

Answers will vary as children make up their own sentences from notes, but all information should be included.

Working with Singular and Plural Form, pages 83-84

Answers will vary according to the way students write the sentences in plural form.

CONTENTS OF THE PLANT RESEARCH UNIT

The beginning lessons in the plant unit are designed for all students to complete. Students will learn to organize given information following outlines. They will also have practice using mindmaps, or webs, to sort out information. They will complete note taking lessons. They will choose activities from an inquiry section of experiments and investigations, according to interests, abilities, and learning styles. They may also choose to do an extra research project on topics related to plants.

For part of the unit, lessons are separated into green and blue strands. Report writing lessons in the green strand section are easier than the lessons in the blue strand. Green strand lessons are for students who are just beginning to learn research skills and note taking, while blue strand lessons are for students who have had some experience, and/or are capable of breaking the information down into more subtopics.

1. Pages 89-90 contain a plant information chart for teachers and students to use, to help understand what has been included in each category for outlining lessons.

2. Pages 91-93 are an organization lesson. Students will learn to organize given information following an outline.

3. Pages 94-101 are four different types of note taking lessons.

4. Pages 102-109 are organization and research lessons following a mindmapping/webbing approach to sort out information.

5. Page 110 gives ideas for research projects on topics related to plants.

6. Pages 111-115 are inquiries for working with plants, based on hands-on experiments and observations.

7. Pages 116-119 are inquiries about plants, based on research and investigations for writing and illustrating.

8. Pages 121-123 are outlines and lists for green strand students to use for taking notes and writing research reports.

9. Pages 125-128 are outlines and lists for blue strand students to use for taking notes and writing research reports.

TEACHER'S GUIDE: PLANT UNIT DIRECTIONS

This unit consists of a great number of possible activities for students to complete, learning research skills, while investigating the plant kingdom. Several different types of research are included. The beginning activities, where students learn to organize information, should be completed by all students. All should spend time on the inquiry section as well, with experiments and observations of plants.

Many of the activities can be done independently, but may also be completed with partners or small groups. The activities can be discussed in cooperative group situations, whenever possible, with many library books available for students to examine together. Encyclopedias or computer printouts should only be used when students cannot find enough information on plants in trade books. Teachers should guide students through these activities, but leave them to think for themselves, or to work cooperatively with peers, as much of the time as they can.

Individuals and cooperative groups can choose from many different types of activities. Some may prefer to follow an outline with note cards to write a report. Some may enjoy using a large piece of butcher paper for an enlarged web, with branches to write their information on. Some may enjoy digging into the inquiry section for ideas to report on, or choose from the list of research topics related to plants.

There are two different strands for part of the unit, for the sake of students with varying abilities. Materials labeled "GREEN" are easier than those labeled "BLUE." Teacher discretion should be used as to which strand each student should follow. Students who have had little experience with note taking and outlining should follow the green strand, unless a teacher feels they would be able to handle the more difficult lessons. Students who have had more experience would benefit from completing the blue strand. See the following directions for an explanation of activities.

NOTE: GREEN STRAND MATERIALS ARE FOUND IN SECTION SIX IN THIS BOOK. BLUE STRAND MATERIALS ARE FOUND IN SECTION SEVEN. MATERIALS NEEDED FOR BOTH STRANDS ARE FOUND IN SECTION FIVE.

Teacher's Guide--Plant Unit Directions (continued)

Pages 89-90

This information chart is included to help teachers and students see what is included in each category used in outlines throughout the plant unit. It includes plant classifications, structures and parts of plants, plant habitats, and life and growth of plants.

Pages 91-93

This lesson is an organization lesson, following an outline. Students are to read the given information, then decide which category on the outline each statement would fit under. Each statement is to be labeled with the number and the letter where it belongs. After all of the statements are labeled, students are to cut them apart with scissors and divide the strips of paper into the three main groups. Within each group, following the outline subtopics, they are to place the strips in a logical order, as if they were going to write a report. The strips are then to be stapled or glued down to a piece of paper and turned in for credit and correction. It is not necessary to write this information in report form, as the purpose is only to learn this type of organization, at this time.

Pages 94-101

These pages are to be used to teach students the skill of note taking. On the first two pages, students will learn to look for the key words and underline them. On the next two pages, they will be asked to write the key words from each statement, as if they were taking notes. The following two pages are to be used to help them organize the information, in note form, under the correct headings. The last two pages are to be used for practice in looking at given notes, and turning the information into complete sentences. Going through these four types of practice is essential before students are asked to take notes.

Pages 102-109

These pages are for a research activity using a mindmapping or webbing approach. Four categories on plants are included, and each web is divided into subtopics. Students are to read information given for each web, then place it on the correct branch of the web. You may decide whether to use this lesson as an organization lesson, and let students write complete statements, or to use it as further practice with note taking, with the information being written in note form on each branch.

This assignment may also be enlarged upon. Individual students might do more research on one or more of the mindmaps. They might use a different color of ink to record information they find themselves, so you can see the extra information they gather, more easily. It can be used for a complete report project, where students organize the information in a logical order, for one or more of the mindmaps, and complete a written report.

You may choose to make this a cooperative group activity, with four groups. Each group could complete one of the mindmaps, gathering as much new material as possible to add to the given information. Findings of each group could then be presented to the entire class, or posted on bulletin boards for everyone to see. Students could also use the jigsaw approach and individually present the findings of their group to the other three groups.

Page 110

This page is included to give students other ideas to use for designing their own research projects. Ideas given include plant pests, plant diseases, plant products, important plant crops, or people who are famous as botanists. Students should also be allowed to come up with their own ideas for extra research projects. If they do, be sure they check with you before they begin working to see if their topic is suitable for research. Information found for these reports should preferably be presented in poster form, then posted for display.

Pages 111-115

These pages include inquiries, using the action verbs from Bloom's Taxonomy, involving higher level thinking skills. All students should spend some time on these activities involving real plants and plant parts. They will be actively involved in experiments or observations. They will grow plants under different conditions, looking for the optimum conditions for proper growth, or examine parts of plants and determine their functions. Most of these projects could be used for full class participation, but they lend themselves to individual, partner, or small group activities. Students should be allowed to choose from these activities according to their interests and learning styles. Findings should be shared with others.

Teacher's Guide--Plant Unit Directions (continued)

Pages 116-119

These pages also include inquiries, using the action verbs from Bloom's Taxonomy, and involve higher-level thinking skills. Students will need to do research to locate answers, then write about or illustrate what they find out about plants. Projects are designed to be completed by individuals, partners, or small groups, according to abilities, interests, and learning styles.

Page 121 (Green Strand)

This page is an outline to be used for research on all plants. It is designed for a complete research report, using note cards for each topic and organizing a final report, according to the order of the outline. Students should try to find information on as many areas as possible that are listed under each topic, then organize their information in a logical order. Students in the green strand will be asked to concentrate on just the four main topics as they take notes. Subtopics given will help them to know what to include for each topic, and will help them with organization. They should put statements on the same subtopic together, and follow the order of the subtopics for the information they have found, as they write their reports.

Page 122 (Green Strand)

This page offers names of specific plants that are well known. They should be the easiest to find in library resources. These plants should be used as topics for specific plant reports. Students should choose the plants they would like to find information on, then follow the outline on page 123.

Page 123 (Green Strand)

This page includes a specific plant outline. It is to be used to help the student organize information for specific plant reports. Note cards should be labeled with each of the four topics, then notes should be taken on each topic. A separate report should be written for each specific plant, following the order of the outline. Students may want to do a series of these as a project, including illustrations of each individual plant.

Teacher's Guide--Plant Unit Directions (continued)

Page 125 (Blue Strand)

This page is an outline to be used by students in the blue strand for research on all plants. It is designed for a complete research report, using note cards for each topic and subtopic, then organizing a final report according to the order of the outline. Blue strand students should take notes on note cards labeled with each subtopic, then use the outline as a guide to determine the order of information when they write their report.

Page 126-127 (Blue Strand)

These pages include names of specific plants that are well known. They should be the easiest to find in library resources. Some plants listed are more uncommon than those for the green strand, and may be a little more difficult to find information on. These plants should be used as topics for specific plant reports. Students should choose the plant or plants they would like to research, then follow the outline given on page 128.

Page 128 (Blue Strand)

This page includes a specific plant outline. It is to be used to help the student organize information for specific plant reports. Note cards should be labeled with each of the four topics, with subdivisions for each of the subtopics. Notes should then be taken on each subtopic. A separate report should be written for each specific plant, following the order of the outline. Students may wish to do a series of these reports as a project, including illustrations of individual plants.

ANSWER KEY: STUDENT WORK PAGES

PLANT UNIT

Organization Lesson, pages 91-93

Students will read and interpret each of the statements and label them to follow the Organization Outline. Answers are as follows:

Note: More than one answer is given for some of the statements, as they may fit more than one category, depending on the interpretation of the student. Let students explain their choices if they see it differently than the given answers.

1. I D
2. I F or III A
3. II A
4. III F
5. I E
6. II D or III B
7. III A
8. III E
9. I B
10. I A
11. II B
12. I G
13. I E
14. III B
15. I C
16. II D
17. III C
18. II C
19. III D
20. I A

21. III B or II D
22. III A
23. I B
24. I C
25. II A or III F
26. II E
27. I D
28. II B
29. III C
30. III D
31. I G
32. II C

Note Taking Practice 1, page 94

Possible Answers (student responses should be similar)

1. Seeds contain stored food-used-growth
2. Seeds grow-roots develop-seek water, minerals
3. Tiny root hairs grow-soil-absorb water, minerals
4. Plants-food-from air-take in-carbon dioxide.
5. Plants make starch, sugar-from carbon, other elements
6. All plants grow-seeds, buds
7. Sepals, green leaves around bud-protect-as it grows
8. Plants-produce food-themselves-long as live
9. Plants-provide nourishment-animals-we eat

ANSWER KEY (continued)

10. Roots-water plants-float-water
11. Mosses-nonflowering-green-live rocks, trees
12. Thallophytes-fungi, bacteria, algae, lichens
13. Club mosses-small, evergreen, seedless-not true mosses
14. Deciduous trees-lose leaves-autumn
15. Seeds cannot grow without-warmth, moisture, oxygen, light
16. Surroundings-plants-live-habitats
17. Groups of plants-same habitat-communities
18. Ferns-temperate climates
19. Liverworts-mosses-moist, shady places
20. Plants-oceans, lakes, rivers, ponds

Note Taking Practice 2, page 95

Possible Answers (student responses should be similar)

1. Most roots-underground-some top of ground
2. Stems useful-supporting leaves, flowers as grow
3. Buds grow-several different places-on stem
4. Points-leaves join stems-nodes
5. Buds may become-flowers, leaves, new branches
6. Some plants-completely underwater, near surface
7. Trees-tropical forests-close together

8. Small seedlings, flowers-on ground under trees
9. Some plants-able-live extreme conditions
10. Plants need-sunlight, precipitation, rich soil-grow
11. Most plants-roots absorb-water-minerals
12. Plants-living organisms-produce own food
13. Carrots, parsnips, beets-large taproots-store food
14. Most plants-pollinated-wind, insects
15. Wind pollinated flowers-usually small, clustered
16. Insect pollinated flowers-bright colors-strong scents
17. Most desert plants-long, deep roots-search water
18. Some plants-parasites-live on other plants-obtain food
19. Plants cannot move about under own power-animals can
20. Ages-trees-determined by counting annual rings

Note Taking Practice 3, page 96

Possible Answers (student responses should be similar)

1. Plants-affected-other plants-same area
2. Chaparrals-covered-thick growths-shrubs, trees
3. Hemlocks, Douglas-firs, cedars-coniferous forests
4. Vines climb-high-trees-rain forests

ANSWER KEY (continued)

5. Chlorophyll-leaves-absorbs sunlight-photosynthesis
6. Majority-plants-leaves-broad, flat
7. Networks veins-carry water throughout leaves
8. Some flowers-series of tiny flowers-look like one
9. Flowers contain reproductive parts-flowering plants
10. All cone-bearing plants-uncovered seeds

Note: For Practice 5 and 6, students may interpret a statement differently, and see it as fitting in another category. Let them explain their reasoning if answers do not fit these answers.

Note Taking Practice 4, page 97

Possible Answers (student responses should be similar)

1. All flowering plants-enclosed seeds
2. Sprouting seeds-germination
3. Water escapes-leaves-goes into air
4. Largest plants-conifers-high-300 feet.
5. Ferns,horsetails-primitive plants-reproduce-spores
6. Lichens grow very slowly-live long time
7. Plants-dark places-need large leaves-catch light
8. Plants-open-need small leaves-due to wind
9. Plants-water-feathery leaves-water passes through
10. Leaves-many leaflets-compound leaves

Note Taking Practice 5, page 98

Notes written will vary, but notes from the following statements should be included under each category:

Description--1, 5, 8

Habitat--2, 6, 7

Plant Life and Growth--3, 4, 9, 10

Note Taking Practice 6, page 99

Notes written will vary, but notes from the following statements should be included under each category:

Description--1, 2, 6

Habitat-4, 7, 9

Plant Life and Growth--3, 5, 8,10

ANSWER KEY *(continued)*

Note Taking Practice 7 and 8, pages 100-101

Answers will vary as children make up their own sentences from these notes, but all of the information should be included.

Mindmapping Lesson, pages 102-109

Students will interpret the given statements for each web, then place the information on the correct branches. The following numbers indicate which statements belong on each branch:

Note: For these organization lessons, students may interpret a statement differently and see it fitting in a different category than the given answers. Let them explain their reasoning if answers do not fit these answers.

Parts of Plants

Seeds--1, 4, 10
Leaves--8, 9, 15
Roots--5, 11, 12
Stems--3, 7, 13
Flowers--2, 6, 14

Habitats of Plants

Forests--1, 10, 11
Water Regions--2, 7, 12
Grasslands--8, 9, 15
Tundra--3, 6, 13
Deserts--4, 5, 14

Kinds of Plants

Thallophytes--1, 8, 12
Bryophytes--2, 11, 15
Pteridophytes--6, 7, 13
Spermatophytes
    Angiosperms--4, 5, 14
Spermatophytes
    Gymnosperms--3, 9, 10

Life and Growth of Plants

Light--1, 6, 12
Food--2, 14, 15
Water--5, 10, 11
Temperature--4, 7, 9
Reproduction--3, 8, 13

SECTION TWO

ANIMAL UNIT

GREEN STRAND MATERIALS

STUDENT CONTRACT

EVIDENCE OF COMPLETING YOUR CONTRACT

RESOURCES--MATERIALS

PROCEDURES

WILD ANIMAL LIST--GREEN

ANIMAL REPORT OUTLINE--GREEN

INFORMATION SHEET: GREEN 1--CHIPMUNK NOTES

ORGANIZATION SHEET: DIRECTIONS FOR CHIPMUNK NOTES

INFORMATION SHEET: GREEN 2--PRAIRIE DOG NOTES

NOTE WRITING PRACTICE PAGES

HOW TO WRITE YOUR ANIMAL RESEARCH REPORT--GREEN

STUDENT CONTRACT
GREEN STRAND

GOALS:

To locate information in library materials
To learn to take notes following an outline
To organize information following an outline
To write a report using the above notes, and following the
    outline

ACTIVITIES:

◊ You will locate information from five different books about a
    wild animal of your choice, and record several sentences
    from each book.

◊ You will follow a simple outline, and using the information
    gathered above, you will be able to label each sentence
    you recorded to indicate which section of the outline it
    fits.

◊ You will write a mini-report using the above information.

◊ Using given information on chipmunks, you will use the
    animal report outline and label each sentence according to
    where it would belong in the outline.

◊ You will cut apart the above information and reorganize it
    into a logical order, following the outline.

◊ You will complete lessons on note taking.

28

◊ You will transfer the information on prairie dogs to note form, using the Note Taking Practice Pages.

◊ Following the outline, you will be able to take notes on a wild animal of your choice, and keep your information separated while you are taking your notes.

◊ You will practice writing sentences in plural form before writing your final report.

◊ You will learn other hints for writing better reports.

◊ Using the outline and the notes you have taken, you will be able to write your information in paragraph form, as a rough draft of an organized report.

◊ You will edit, revise, and proofread your rough draft.

◊ You will write your final report.

◊ You will complete a bibliography, pictures, and a cover for your report.

EVIDENCE OF COMPLETING YOUR CONTRACT

GREEN STRAND

1. Worksheets 1 and 2 completed along with a mini-report written from this information.

2. Chipmunk assignment completed.

3. Note taking lessons completed.

4. Information on prairie dogs transferred to note writing practice pages, in note form.

5. Note taking hints read.

6. Notes completed on a wild animal of your choice.

7. Plural writing practice pages completed.

8. Report writing hints, and editing, revising, and proofreading hints, read.

9. Rough draft completed, edited, revised, and proofread.

10. Final report written, including a bibliography page, pictures, and a cover.

EACH OF THE ABOVE ASSIGNMENTS SHOULD BE TURNED IN AS IT IS COMPLETED!

RESOURCES--MATERIALS

GREEN STRAND

1. A great quantity of books will be needed to help you fulfill this contract. Books from home, school libraries, or other libraries are permissible. Remember to list them on your Bibliography card.

2. Films or videos on a variety of wild animals may be shown during the time you are doing this research. Filmstrips may also be available. You should take notes on your animal if it is covered in these materials. Be sure to include the name of the film, video, or filmstrip on your Bibliography card.

3. **ENCYCLOPEDIAS ARE OFF LIMITS!!!!!!!!!!** You are learning to organize information taken from various sources. Encyclopedias usually have it organized ahead of time and you would not learn what you are trying to learn if you use them.

PROCEDURES

GREEN STRAND

1. Choose a wild animal from the list provided. Using library books, locate your animal in at least five different books.

HINT: THINK! Don't just go looking in any book for your animal. Here are some clues to help you.

   A. LOOK AT THE TITLE! Would you be apt to find a lion in a book about insects? Use the title first to help you determine which books appear to have information on your animal.

   B. LOOK FOR AN INDEX! If the title doesn't help, see if there is an index at the back of the book. This is a great place to look because, if your book does have an index, it will even tell you what page or pages to look at for information about your animal.

   C. LOOK FOR A TABLE OF CONTENTS! Read through the chapter titles. Sometimes items contained in chapters will be listed.

   D. LOOK THROUGH THE PAGES! If you can't tell from the title and the book doesn't have an index, or a table of contents, you may have to skim through the pages. Only do this if the title appears to be one that would include your animal.

2. As you locate information on your animal, write down the title of the book, the author's name, and the page number or numbers where the information is found. (Use Worksheets One and Two, pages 72-73.)

3. Copy two or three sentences about your animal from each book. (Use Worksheets One and Two, pages 72-73.) You should have ten to fifteen sentences of information to use for the next activity. Look for information to describe your animal, to tell what it eats, where its home is located, what the young are like, and/or how it protects itself.

4. Look over the outline provided, Animal Report Outline-Green, page 38. Using this outline, label each of your sentences according to the section under which it should fit.

Example:

Squirrels, when hungry, will eat acorns, nuts, seeds, berries, or grubs. (III. Food--A. What Food They Eat)

Chipmunks are friendly, noisy little creatures and will often come near. (I. Description--B. How the Animals Act)

5. Write a mini-report, following your outline, using the information you have written on Worksheets One and Two. Write sentences about description first, then those about home, then food, etc. As you write, try to follow the order of your subtopics under each section, whenever it is possible. You may have to skip an area if you don't have any information on it.

6. Locate the following materials:

   <u>For a Chipmunk Labeling Activity</u>
   Animal Report Outline-Green, page 38
   Information Sheet: Green-1, page 39
   Organization Sheet: Green, page 40

7. Organize the chipmunk information according to the directions given on the organization sheet, and turn in your pasted strips for correction.

8. Complete the note taking lessons found on pages 74-81. (Note Taking Sheets 1-8)

9. Read "Note Taking: Hints for Students," page 82.

10. Find the information on the Prairie Dog, Information Sheet: Green-2, page 41. Change it to note form and record it on the Note Writing Practice Pages--Green 1-4, pages 42-45.

NOW YOU ARE READY TO BEGIN YOUR FINAL REPORT!
PLEASE FOLLOW THE DIRECTIONS
VERY CAREFULLY!

11. Using your outline and note cards, label each note card with one section of the outline on each card. Use your topics and main subtopics.

    Card One--Description (What the animals look like)
    Card Two--Description (How the animals act)
    Card Three--Home (Where the homes are located)
    Card Four--Home (What the homes are like)

Continue labeling cards until you have one card for each section of your outline. Also label one card as a Bibliography card, a place to keep track of the books and page numbers you will be using for your report.

NOW YOU ARE READY
TO TAKE NOTES ON
YOUR FAVORITE ANIMAL
FOR YOUR FINAL REPORT!

Choose an animal from the list provided. Write its name at the top of your first card. Be sure to choose an animal that you really want to learn more about so you will truly enjoy doing your report.

HEAD FOR THOSE
LIBRARY BOOKS AGAIN!

This time, however, study each sentence you read before you write it down. Decide which part of the outline it fits and then write it on the card that you have labeled for that topic. Do not write the complete sentence. Use just enough words so that you will understand how to use this information to make complete sentences for your report. You may use phrases to help you remember information, or write it in your own words.

BE CAREFUL! BE SURE WHAT YOU WRITE DOWN HAS THE
SAME MEANING AS WHAT YOU'VE READ. ALSO, DO NOT
WRITE DOWN ANYTHING EXCEPT WHAT YOU FIND IN THE
BOOKS. THIS IS RESEARCH!

Be sure to remember to write the name of each book that you use and the page numbers on your bibliography card. Also, try very hard to get information on each of your note cards.

12. As soon as you have enough sentences to meet your contract agreement, and information on most of your cards, it is time to learn more about writing your report.

13. Read "Report Writing: Hints for Students," page 85.

14. Complete "Working with Singular and Plural Form," pages 83-84.

15. Follow "How to Write Your Animal Research Report-Green," page 46, in order to write your rough draft.

16. Edit, revise, and proofread your rough draft. Read "Editing, Revising, and Proofreading: Hints for Students," page 86, before you begin.

17. Write your final draft. Follow "How to Finish Your Animal Research Report," page 87.

18. Turn in your notes, your rough draft, and the final copy of your report for correction.

WILD ANIMAL LIST
Green

Please choose an animal from this list for your report. They will be easier to find information on than other animals you might choose, because they are more common.

ALLIGATOR	KANGAROO	SKUNK
BAT	KOALA	SQUIRREL
BEAR	LION	TIGER
BEAVER	OPOSSUM	TOAD
CAMEL	OTTER	TORTOISE
CROCODILE	PORCUPINE	TURTLE
DEER	RABBIT	WALRUS
ELEPHANT	RACCOON	WEASEL
FOX	RATTLESNAKE	WHALE
FROG	SEAL	WOLF

ANIMAL REPORT OUTLINE
Green

I. DESCRIPTION

    A. WHAT THE ANIMALS LOOK LIKE
       (family trait, color, size, shape)

    B. HOW THE ANIMALS ACT
       (personality, behavior)

II. HOME

    A. WHERE THE HOMES ARE LOCATED
       (continent, country, forest, field, etc.)

    B. WHAT THE HOMES ARE LIKE
       (how they look, how they are made, how they are cared for)

III. FOOD

    A. WHAT FOOD THEY EAT
       (can be a list of items)

    B. HOW THEY GET THEIR FOOD
       (collecting, storing)

IV. PROTECTION

    A. WHAT THEIR ENEMIES ARE

    B. HOW THE ANIMALS PROTECT THEMSELVES
       (temper, coloration, strength)

V. YOUNG

    A. HOW THE BABIES DEVELOP

    B. WHAT THE BABIES LOOK LIKE

    C. HOW THE BABIES ARE CARED FOR

INFORMATION SHEET: GREEN 1

CHIPMUNK NOTES

Chipmunks keep house together.

Chipmunks are always hungry.

Chipmunk dens are underground burrows.

Chipmunks weigh about 3 to 5 ounces.

Berries are the chipmunks' favorite food.

Chipmunks often crouch low and lie still to defend themselves.

Chipmunks are both shy and curious.

Chipmunks settle down for the winter, and plug up their doors with dirt.

Chipmunks' tails are almost as long as their bodies.

They are noisy, cheerful, friendly little creatures.

They can carry prune pits in their pouches.

Chipmunks store their food.

Chipmunks eat beetles, corn, blueberries, mushrooms, snails, etc.

They live in a space of about two acres.

The weasel is the worst enemy chipmunks have.

Chipmunks swim if they must.

ORGANIZATION SHEET: GREEN

HOW TO ORGANIZE THE CHIPMUNK INFORMATION

1. Read each of the statements about chipmunks.

2. Read your animal report outline.

3. Reread the statements about chipmunks, and label each one according to which part of the outline the information should fit under.

   Example: Chipmunks live all over the United States.
   (II. Home--A. Where The Homes Are Located)

4. After each statement is labeled, use scissors and cut the statements apart. Be careful! Don't lose any of your strips of paper.

5. Separate your strips into piles labeled Description, Home, Food, Protection, and Young.

6. Start with the strips on description. Read them carefully. Rearrange them into a logical order for a paragraph on description. If possible, separate them into subtopics on what the animal looks like, and how it acts.

7. Glue, tape, or staple these strips down to a complete piece of paper, after you have them in a logical order.

8. Continue in the same way with Home, Food, etc.

9. Turn in your sheet of organized strips for correction.

PRAIRIE DOG NOTES

Prairie dogs are chunky, short-legged, yellowish-brown rodents.

Prairie dogs call each other with alarm calls when danger is near.

The burrows of prairie dogs are elaborate bunches of tunnels with different rooms, but each burrow only has one outside entrance.

Their babies are from about two to three and a half inches long when they are born, but they grow fast.

They are found on open plains in North America from Canada to Mexico.

Prairie dogs make chirping noises and noises that sound like barks.

When one sounds an alarm, they all run for cover into the nearest burrow.

Prairie dogs will be out looking for food on a nice day in the winter.

They are slightly smaller than house cats.

Enemies of prairie dogs are snakes, coyotes, hawks, eagles, foxes, badgers, etc.

Prairie dogs eat grasses, grasshoppers, and other insects.

Prairie dogs do not hibernate, but they live on fat stored in their bodies to help them get through cold weather.

Prairie dog babies have to leave their burrows when they are about three years old and find a burrow for themselves.

Prairie dogs dig their burrows by loosening the dirt with their front feet, then kicking it backward with their hind feet.

NOTE WRITING PRACTICE: GREEN 1

I. DESCRIPTION

    A. WHAT THE ANIMALS LOOK LIKE
       (family trait, color, size, shape)

    B. HOW THE ANIMALS ACT (personality, behavior)

NOTE WRITING PRACTICE: GREEN 2

II. HOMES

   A. WHERE THE HOMES ARE LOCATED
      (continent, country, forest, field)

   B. WHAT THE HOMES ARE LIKE
      (how they look, how they are made, how they are cared for)

III. FOOD

   A. WHAT FOOD THEY EAT

B. HOW THEY GET THEIR FOOD
(collecting, storing)

IV. PROTECTION

A. WHAT THEIR ENEMIES ARE

B. HOW THE ANIMALS PROTECT THEMSELVES
(temper, coloration, strength)

NOTE WRITING PRACTICE: GREEN 4

V. YOUNG

    A. HOW THE BABIES DEVELOP

    B. WHAT THE BABIES LOOK LIKE

    C. HOW THE BABIES ARE CARED FOR

HOW TO WRITE YOUR ANIMAL RESEARCH REPORT--GREEN

Write your title at the top of your page, then write a set of continuing paragraphs, one for each topic in your outline. DO NOT LABEL YOUR PARAGRAPH TOPICS IN YOUR REPORT. Just indent and start a new paragraph for each topic.

Description

Start with these cards. Write a paragraph for A, "What They Look Like." Try to keep ideas on family trait together, then shape, size, etc. Then indent and write another paragraph for B, "How They Act." Section B should have ideas on personality first, then behavior.

Food

Again, be sure to write at least two different paragraphs, one for what food they eat and one for how they get their food. Keep ideas on collecting food together before you write about storing of food.

Home

Follow above instructions, with at least one paragraph for each topic you have information for. Skip an area if it does not fit your animal.

Protection

Write two different paragraphs again, if possible. If your animal doesn't have many enemies and you don't have much information, this could be written as one paragraph.

Young

First, write about how the baby develops. Your first paragraph should include ideas about life cycles, eggs, live babies, etc. Your second paragraph should describe the baby with ideas on shape, color, size, etc., while your third paragraph should tell about how the baby is cared for, including feeding and protection.

SECTION THREE

ANIMAL UNIT

BLUE STRAND MATERIALS

STUDENT CONTRACT

EVIDENCE OF COMPLETING YOUR CONTRACT

RESOURCES--MATERIALS

PROCEDURES

WILD ANIMAL LIST--BLUE

INFORMATION SHEETS: BLUE 1-2--BUTTERFLY NOTES

ORGANIZATION SHEET: DIRECTIONS FOR BUTTERFLY NOTES

INFORMATION SHEETS: BLUE 3-4--SPIDER NOTES

NOTE WRITING PRACTICE PAGES--BLUE

HOW TO WRITE YOUR ANIMAL RESEARCH REPORT--BLUE

STUDENT CONTRACT
BLUE STRAND

GOALS:

To locate information in library materials
To learn to take notes following an outline
To organize information following an outline
To write a report using the above notes, and following the
   outline

ACTIVITIES:

◊ You will locate information from five different books about a
   wild animal of your choice, and record several sentences
   from each book.

◊ You will follow a simple outline, and using the information
   gathered above, you will be able to label each sentence
   you recorded to indicate which section of the outline it
   fits.

◊ You will write a mini-report using the above information.

◊ Using given information on butterflies, you will use the
   animal report outline and label each sentence according
   to where it would belong in the outline.

◊ You will cut apart the above information and reorganize it
   into a logical order, following the outline.

◊ You will complete lessons on note taking.

48

◊ You will transfer the information on spiders to note form, using the Note Taking Practice Pages.

◊ Following the outline, you will be able to take notes on a wild animal of your choice, and keep your information separated while you are taking your notes.

◊ You will practice writing sentences in plural form before writing your final report.

◊ You will learn other hints for writing better reports.

◊ Using the outline and the notes you have taken, you will be able to write your information in paragraph form as a rough draft of an organized report.

◊ You will edit, revise, and proofread your rough draft.

◊ You will write your final report.

◊ You will complete a bibliography, pictures, and a cover for your report.

EVIDENCE OF COMPLETING YOUR CONTRACT

BLUE STRAND

1. Worksheets 1 and 2 completed along with a mini-report written from this information.

2. Butterfly assignment completed.

3. Note taking lessons completed.

4. Information on spiders transferred to note writing practice pages, in note form.

5. Note taking hints read.

6. Notes completed on a wild animal of your choice.

7. Plural writing practice pages completed.

8. Report writing hints, and editing, revising, and proofreading hints, read.

9. Rough draft completed, edited, revised, and proofread.

10. Final report written, including a bibliography page, pictures, and a cover.

EACH OF THE ABOVE ASSIGNMENTS SHOULD BE TURNED IN AS IT IS COMPLETED!

RESOURCES--MATERIALS
BLUE STRAND

1. A great quantity of books will be needed to help you fulfill this contract. Books from home, school libraries, or other libraries are permissible. Remember to list them on your Bibliography card.

2. Films or videos on a variety of wild animals may be shown during the time you are doing this research. Filmstrips may also be available. You should take notes on your animal if it is covered in these materials. Be sure to include the name of the film, video, or filmstrip on your Bibliography card.

3. **ENCYCLOPEDIAS ARE OFF LIMITS!!!!!!!!!** You are learning to organize information taken from various sources. Encyclopedias usually have it organized ahead of time and you would not learn what you are trying to learn if you use them.

PROCEDURES
BLUE STRAND

1. Choose a wild animal from the list provided. Using library books, locate your animal in at least five different books.

HINT: THINK! Don't just go looking in any book for your animal. Here are some clues to help you.

A. LOOK AT THE TITLE! Would you be apt to find a lion in a book about insects? Use the title first to help you determine which books appear to have information on your animal.

B. LOOK FOR AN INDEX! If the title doesn't help, see if there is an index at the back of the book. This is a great place to look because, if your book does have an index, it will even tell you what page or pages to look at for information about your animal.

C. LOOK FOR A TABLE OF CONTENTS! Read through the chapter titles. Sometimes items contained in chapters will be listed.

D. LOOK THROUGH THE PAGES! If you can't tell from the title and the book doesn't have an index, or a table of contents, you may have to skim through the pages. Only do this if the title appears to be one that would include your animal.

2. As you locate information on your animal, write down the title of the book, the author's name, and the page number or numbers where the information is found. (Use Worksheets One and Two, pages 72-73.)

3. Copy three or four sentences about your animal from each book. (Use Worksheets One and Two, pages 72-73.) You should have fifteen to twenty sentences of information to use for the next activity. Look for information to describe your animal, to tell what it eats, where its home is located, what the young are like, and/or how it protects itself.

4. Look over the outline provided, Animal Report Outline-Blue, pages 58-59. Using this outline, label each of your sentences according to the section under which it should fit.

Example:

Squirrels, when hungry, will eat acorns, nuts, seeds, berries, or grubs. (III. Food--A. What Food They Eat)

Chipmunks are friendly, noisy little creatures and will often come near.
(I. Description--B. How the Animals Act
1. Personality)

5. Write a mini-report, following your outline, using the information you have written on Worksheets One and Two. Write sentences about Description A first, then Description B, then those about Home A, Home B, then Food A, Food B, etc. As you write, include information about your subtopics according to the order given in the outline. You may have to skip an area if you don't have any information on it.

53

6. Locate the following materials:

   For a Butterfly Labeling Activity
        Animal Report Outline-Blue, pages 58-59
        Information Sheets: Blue-1-2, pages 60-61
        Organization Sheet: Blue, page 62

7. Organize the butterfly information according to the directions given on the organization sheet, and turn in your pasted strips for correction.

8. Complete the note taking lessons found on pages 74-81. (Note Taking Sheets 1-8)

9. Read "Note Taking: Hints for Students," page 82.

10. Find the information on the Spider, Information Sheets: Blue-3-4, pages 63-64. Change it to note form and record it on the Note Writing Practice Pages--Blue 1-5, pages 65-69.

NOW YOU ARE READY TO BEGIN YOUR FINAL REPORT! PLEASE FOLLOW THE DIRECTIONS VERY CAREFULLY!

11. Using your outline and note cards, label each note card with one section of the outline on each card. Use your topics and main subtopics. You may wish to use a note card for each subtopic.

    Card One--Description (What the animals look like)
    Card Two--Description (How the animals act)
    Card Three--Home (Where the homes are located)
    Card Four--Home (What the homes are like)

Continue labeling cards until you have one card for each section of your outline. Also label one card as a Bibliography card, a place to keep track of the books and page numbers you will be using for your report.

NOW YOU ARE READY TO TAKE NOTES ON YOUR FAVORITE ANIMAL FOR YOUR FINAL REPORT!

Choose an animal from the list provided. Write its name at the top of your first card. Be sure to choose an animal that you really want to learn more about so you will truly enjoy doing your report.

HEAD FOR THOSE LIBRARY BOOKS AGAIN!

This time, however, study each sentence you read before you write it down. Decide which part of the outline it fits and then write it on the card that you have labeled for that topic. Do not write the complete sentence. Use just enough words so that you will understand how to use this information to make complete sentences for your report. You may use phrases to help you remember information, or you may write it in your own words.

BE CAREFUL! BE SURE WHAT YOU WRITE DOWN HAS THE SAME MEANING AS WHAT YOU'VE READ. ALSO, DO NOT WRITE DOWN ANYTHING EXCEPT WHAT YOU FIND IN THE BOOKS. THIS IS RESEARCH!

Be sure to remember to write the name of each book that you use and the page numbers on your bibliography card. Also, try very hard to get information on each of your note cards.

12. As soon as you have enough sentences to meet your contract agreement, and information on most of your cards, it is time to learn more about writing your report.

13. Read "Report Writing: Hints for Students," page 85.

14. Complete "Working with Singular and Plural Form," pages 83-84.

15. Follow "How to Write Your Animal Research Report-Blue," page 70, in order to write your rough draft.

16. Edit, revise and proofread your rough draft. Read "Editing, Revising, and Proofreading: Hints for Students," page 86, before you begin.

17. Write your final draft. Follow "How to Finish Your Animal Research Report," page 87.

18. Turn in your notes, your rough draft, and the final copy of your report for correction.

WILD ANIMAL LIST
Blue

Please choose an animal from this list for your report. These will be easier to find information on than other animals you might choose, because they are more common.

ALLIGATOR	BAT	BEAR	SHARK
OTTER	HYENA	CHEETAH	OSTRICH
PORCUPINE	CARP	OWL	STARFISH
LADYBUG	DOLPHIN	BEAVER	RATTLESNAKE
CHIPMUNK	KANGAROO	KOALA	OPOSSUM
RABBIT	RAY	EEL	DEER
SAND DOLLAR	SALMON	EAGLE	DUCK
WOLF	SEAL	RACCOON	CRICKET
SKUNK	TORTOISE	TURTLE	SQUIRREL
WOLVERINE	TIGER	TOAD	ELEPHANT
HERON	FROG	WALRUS	SEA URCHIN
LIZARD	SNAKE	BEE	EARTHWORM
TERMITE	ANT	DRAGONFLY	GRASSHOPPER
PELICAN	MOTH	WHALE	HUMMINGBIRD
WEASEL	FOX	PENGUIN	CROCODILE

ANIMAL REPORT OUTLINE
Blue

I. DESCRIPTION

    A. WHAT THE ANIMALS LOOK LIKE
        1. FAMILY TRAIT
        2. SHAPE
        3. SIZE
        4. COLOR

    B. HOW THE ANIMALS ACT
        1. PERSONALITY
        2. BEHAVIOR

II. HOMES

    A. WHERE THE HOMES ARE LOCATED
        1. CONTINENT
        2. COUNTRY
        3. FOREST, FIELD, ETC.

    B. WHAT THE HOMES ARE LIKE
        1. HOW THEY LOOK
        2. HOW THEY ARE MADE
        3. HOW THEY ARE CARED FOR

III. FOOD

    A. WHAT FOOD THEY EAT (can be a list of items)

    B. HOW THEY GET THEIR FOOD
        1. COLLECTING
        2. STORING

IV. PROTECTION

    A. WHAT THEIR ENEMIES ARE

    B. HOW THE ANIMALS PROTECT THEMSELVES
        1. COLORATION
        2. TEMPER
        3. STRENGTH

V. YOUNG

    A. HOW THE BABIES DEVELOP

    B. WHAT THE BABIES LOOK LIKE

    C. HOW THE BABIES ARE CARED FOR

BUTTERFLY NOTES

Butterflies have big, colorful wings, covered with scales.

Butterflies are insects.

They have six legs and their bodies have three parts; a head, a thorax, and an abdomen.

Nearly all butterflies fly only in the daytime.

About 16,000 kinds of butterflies are known in the world.

The most beautiful butterflies are found in forests in hot, tropical regions.

Butterflies fold their wings when resting on any object.

The antennas of butterflies end in little knobs.

The scales of butterflies give them their beautiful colors.

Butterflies live entirely on liquids, such as nectar, a sweet liquid found in flowers.

Butterflies depend on flowering plants for food.

Enemies of butterflies are birds, wasps, flies, praying mantises, and spiders.

Some butterflies migrate according to the seasons of the year.

Some butterflies pass the winter asleep in sheltered places such as hollow logs.

BUTTERFLY NOTES (continued)

Some butterflies are protected by their coloring.

Some butterflies are evil-tasting so that once a bird has tasted one, he will never taste another.

About 700 different kinds of butterflies are known in North America.

Butterflies have a long coiled tube for a mouth, through which they suck their food.

The young of butterflies are called caterpillars.

Butterflies go through several stages of growth, during which they change their forms.

Caterpillars turn into butterflies.

Caterpillars have jaws for biting solid food.

Caterpillars enclose themselves in a cocoon while they go through the pupa stage.

Caterpillars protect themselves best by feeding only at night and hiding during the day.

In the spring butterflies emerge from the cocoons.

Adult butterflies are completely harmless.

A single butterfly may lay as many as a thousand eggs.

Scales are arranged on the wings of butterflies like shingles on a roof.

ORGANIZATION SHEET: BLUE

HOW TO ORGANIZE THE BUTTERFLY INFORMATION

1. Read each of the statements about butterflies.

2. Read your animal report outline.

3. Reread the statements about butterflies, and label each one according to which part of the outline the information should fit under.

   Example: Butterflies go through stages as they grow.
   (V. Young--A. Development)

4. After each statement is labeled, use scissors and cut the statements apart. Be careful! Don't lose any of your strips of paper.

5. Separate your strips into piles labeled Description, Home, Food, Protection, and Young.

6. Start with the strips you have on description and separate them into groups for what the animal looks like and how it acts. Then separate the strips for what it looks like into family, shape, size, color, and other. Separate the strips on how it acts into those on personality and those on behavior.

7. Glue, tape, or staple these strips down to a complete piece of paper, after you have them in a logical order.

8. Continue in the same way with Home, Food, etc.

9. Turn in your sheet of organized strips for correction.

INFORMATION SHEET: BLUE 3

SPIDER NOTES

Spiders' webs trap insects that fly into them.

Spiders are egg-laying animals.

Spiders' bodies have only two parts--a front part called the cephalothorax, and a back part called the abdomen.

Some people think spiders are insects, but they are not.

All four of the spiders' sets of legs are attached to their front sections.

Spiders eat insects.

Spiders belong to a group of animals called arachnids.

Spiders have glands contained in their rear sections with which to spin the silk they need for their webs.

Spiders have four pairs of legs, or eight legs, while insects only have six legs.

Spiders live in their webs.

The front body section contains the head and the poison fangs a spider uses to paralyze its prey.

Spiders eat flies, grasshoppers, locusts, plant lice, aphids, and other insects that are harmful to plants.

Baby spiders hatch, looking just like adult spiders, but smaller.

Spider eggs look like tiny white pearls.

Spiders can control insects larger than themselves, because they can paralyze them and wrap them with silk.

63

SPIDER NOTES (continued)

Female spiders usually die right after laying their eggs.

There are thousands of different kinds of spiders.

Spiders spin a web over food they catch if they aren't ready to eat it.

Spiders must have soft food so they can eat it without chewing.

The largest spider measures about 7 inches across.

Insect-eating mammals will also eat spiders.

The spiders' "arms" are not used for walking, but only for grasping objects and holding on to them while they paralyze them.

A single female spider may lay more than a thousand eggs.

Some spiders do not spin webs, but live in the ground instead.

Spiders spin a casing of silk to protect the eggs they lay.

Moles and shrews will feed on spiders when they find them.

Several poison bites from a spider will kill an insect.

Most spiders can take care of themselves as soon as they hatch.

Spiders shed their hard outer shells several times while growing.

Newly hatched spiders can spin silk immediately.

Baby spiders may eat each other after they hatch.

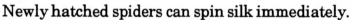

NOTE WRITING PRACTICE: BLUE 1

I. DESCRIPTION

   A. WHAT THE ANIMALS LOOK LIKE

      1. FAMILY

      2. SHAPE

      3. SIZE

      4. COLOR

      5. OTHER

NOTE WRITING PRACTICE: BLUE 2

B. HOW THE ANIMALS ACT

  1. PERSONALITY

  2. BEHAVIOR

II. HOME

  A. WHERE THE HOMES ARE LOCATED

  1. CONTINENT

  2. COUNTRY

  3. FOREST, FIELD, ETC.

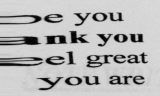

ARE LIKE

OK

2. HOW THEY ARE MADE

3. HOW THEY ARE CARED FOR

III. FOOD

    A. WHAT FOOD THEY EAT

    B. HOW THEY GET THEIR FOOD

       1. COLLECTING

       2. STORING

NOTE WRITING PRACTICE: BLUE 4

IV. PROTECTION

    A. WHAT THEIR ENEMIES ARE

    B. HOW THE ANIMALS PROTECT THEMSELVES

        1. COLORATION

        2. TEMPER

        3. STRENGTH

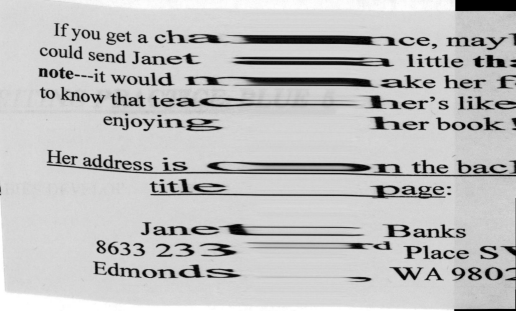

NOTE W...

V. YOUNG

   A. HOW THE BA...

   B. WHAT THE BABIES LOOK LIKE

   C. HOW THE BABIES ARE CARED FOR

HOW TO WRITE YOUR ANIMAL RESEARCH REPORT--BLUE

Write your title at the top of your page, then write a set of continuing paragraphs, one for each topic or subtopic in your outline. DO NOT LABEL YOUR PARAGRAPH TOPICS IN YOUR REPORT Just indent and start a new paragraph for each new topic or subtopic.

Description

Start with these cards. Write at least one paragraph for "A. What They Look Like." If you have enough notes, make separate paragraphs for family trait, size, color, and/or shape, or you may combine them in two if necessary. Then indent and write another paragraph for "B. How They Act." Do not mix "A" and "B" even if you only have one sentence for one of these topics.

Food

Again, be sure to have at least two different paragraphs, one for what they eat and one for how they get their food. Collecting and storing should be separated if you have enough notes.

Home

Follow above instructions, with at least one paragraph for each topic you have information for. Skip an area if it does not fit your animal.

Protection

You should have at least two different paragraphs, if possible. If your animal has almost no enemies and doesn't need protection, this may be written as one paragraph.

Young

Your first paragraph should include facts about how the animal reproduces, life cycles, eggs, live babies, etc. Your second paragraph should describe the baby with size, shape, color, etc. Your third paragraph should contain facts about how the baby is cared for, including feeding and protection.

SECTION FOUR

ANIMAL UNIT

MATERIALS FOR ALL STUDENTS

WORKSHEETS 1-2

NOTE TAKING SHEETS 1-2--UNDERLINING KEY WORDS

NOTE TAKING SHEETS 3-4--WRITING KEY WORDS

NOTE TAKING SHEETS 5-6
WRITING NOTES UNDER CORRECT HEADINGS

NOTE TAKING SHEETS 7-8
CHANGING NOTES TO SENTENCE FORM

NOTE TAKING: HINTS FOR STUDENTS

WORKING WITH SINGULAR AND PLURAL FORM

REPORT WRITING: HINTS FOR STUDENTS

EDITING, REVISING, AND PROOFREADING:
HINTS FOR STUDENTS

HOW TO FINISH YOUR ANIMAL RESEARCH REPORT

NAME_____

ANIMAL_____

1. BOOK_____

AUTHOR_____PAGE_____

2. BOOK_____

AUTHOR_____PAGE_____

3. BOOK_____

    AUTHOR_____PAGE_____

4. BOOK_____

    AUTHOR_____PAGE_____

5. BOOK_____

    AUTHOR_____PAGE_____

NOTE TAKING SHEET 1

Underline the key words in the following statements:

SNAILS

1. Many kinds of snails live in the sea.

2. Snails belong to the mollusk family.

3. Snails have a foot which helps them to move.

4. The largest snails live in tropical climates.

5. Most snails live in spiral-shaped or cone-shaped shells.

6. There are thousands of different kinds of snails.

7. Snails have soft bodies without backbones.

8. Snails live in ponds, fresh water rivers and lakes, and on land.

TAPIRS

1. Tapirs are usually timid and try to stay away from people.

2. Tapirs are heavy, thick-set animals with tiny tails and short legs.

3. Tapirs have long noses and upper lips resembling the trunk of an elephant.

4. Tapirs eat leaves or twigs.

5. Tapirs are pig-like mammals.

6. Tapirs travel alone or in groups of two or three.

NOTE TAKING SHEET 2

Underline the key words in the following statements:

SNAKES

1. Snakes are reptiles or crawling animals.

2. Snakes make their homes in trees and under bushes, in crevices of rocks, and under the ground.

3. Snakes may live in hot deserts, high mountains, lowlands, or the sea.

4. Snakes are long, slender animals with backbones and ribs and scales.

5. Snakes can move very quickly.

6. Snakes often shed their skins while growing, and get new ones.

7. Snakes eat frogs, toads, insects, rats, mice, rabbits, birds, and fish.

KOALAS

1. Koalas are found on the continent of Australia.

2. Koalas do not have tails.

3. The leaves of the eucalyptus tree are the koalas' main food.

4. Koalas are marsupials.

5. Koalas spend most of their time high up in eucalyptus trees.

6. Koalas' pouches are pockets of skin on their abdomens.

7. Koalas are good climbers.

NOTE TAKING SHEET 3

Write the key words from the following in note form:

JAGUARS

1. Jaguars are found in hot, tropical areas from South Texas and Mexico through Argentina.

_____

2. Jaguars look like leopards.

_____

3. Jaguars can be up to 7 feet long and weigh up to 200 pounds.

_____

4. Jaguars are big spotted animals.

_____

5. Jaguars belong to the cat family.

_____

6. Jaguars may cover several hundred miles as they travel.

_____

7. Jaguars will attack horses and cattle, or even a man.

_____

8. Most jaguars travel alone.

_____

NOTE TAKING SHEET 4

Write the key words from the following in note form:

MUSKRATS

1. Muskrats look like large field mice.

_____

2. Female muskrats may have 2 to 6 babies at a time.

_____

3. Muskrats belong to the rodent family and are gnawing animals.

_____

4. Muskrats eat tiny animals found in the water, as well as grass and seeds.

_____

5. Muskrats' nests usually have underwater entrances.

_____

6. Their relatives are rats, squirrels, and beavers.

_____

7. Muskrats live in and around swamps and lakes in many parts of the United States.

_____

77

NOTE TAKING SHEET 5

Put the following information under the correct heading, in note form:

Description

Home

Food

LIONS

1. Lions are large, fierce members of the cat family.
2. Lions live together and travel together through savannas.
3. Lions feed on antelope, zebra, and bush pigs.
4. They are very clever when stalking their prey.
5. Lions' tails are about three feet long, ending in a tuft of bushy hair.
6. Lions have short hair that is usually yellowish-brown.
7. Male lions have manes, long hair growing around their necks.
8. Lions will eat whatever game is easy to find.
9. Lions are found in much of Africa, and in parts of Southwest Asia.
10. Lions are usually 8-11 feet long and weigh from 400-600 pounds.
11. They stalk their prey very silently, or lie in wait at drinking and feeding places.
12. Lions can kill small animals with one blow of the paw.
13. They are good hunters, and usually hunt at night.
14. Many lions live in savannahs south of the Sahara Desert in Africa.

Put the following information under the correct heading, in note form:

<u>Description</u>

<u>Home</u>

<u>Food</u>

FROGS

1. Some frogs live in water, and some live on land.
2. Frogs are good swimmers due to their webbed hind feet.
3. Frogs range from 1-12 inches in length.
4. There are hundreds of different kinds of frogs.
5. Frogs' tongues snap out very quickly to catch insects for food.
6. Frogs are found all over the world.
7. They move by hopping with their strong hind legs.
8. Most frogs have teeth in their upper jaws.
9. Frogs live in forests, fields, swamps, and ponds.
10. Frogs don't chew their food, and usually swallow it whole.
11. If their food is almost too large to swallow whole, they use their front feet to push it down their throats.
12. Most frogs live near the water on swampy ground.
13. Some frogs live in trees and some live in underground burrows.
14. Frogs capture live food, usually insects, with their long, sticky tongues.

Change the following notes to sentence form:

BOBCAT

Three feet long, including tail

_____

Fifteen to thirty pounds

_____

Eat small birds, deer or fawns, mammals

_____

Live in forests, mountains, deserts, swamps

_____

No natural enemies

_____

Excellent hunters, hunt at night

_____

Have razor sharp claws and needle-like teeth

_____

Live throughout North America

_____

NOTE TAKING SHEET 8

Change the following notes to sentence form:

RED FOX

Bodies including heads-30 inches, tail-14 inches

_____

8-10 pounds

_____

Live in brushy areas, woodlands, treeless areas

_____

Eat quail, ducks, rabbits, pheasants, poultry, frogs, snakes

_____

Enemies--lynx, owls, hawks, mountain lions, wolves, bobcats

_____

Long, sharp noses, pointed ears, bright yellow eyes

_____

Litters--six to eight pups, fully furred, blind at first

_____

Males sleep outside during winter, females in dens

_____

NOTE TAKING:
HINTS FOR STUDENTS

1. Know what information you are looking for.

2. Skim and scan material you believe will have what you are looking for. Watch titles, look at indexes and tables of contents.

3. Read carefully when you find your information.

4. Do not write down the name of the animal except as a title, as doing so is just a waste of time.

5. Write only key words that you will be able to turn back into sentences. Do not copy complete sentences, but be sure you understand what you write down.

6. Try very hard to find information on each topic and subtopic.

7. Be careful changing notes to your own words. Be sure the meaning is still the same as what you read.

8. Take notes carefully on each topic and put them on note cards that are labeled with each topic.

9. If information belongs in two places on your note cards, separate it in half if you can. Otherwise, write it in both places. You can decide where to use it later.

10. Be sure to take notes from at least five different sources. Do not use encyclopedias or books that have each of your topics listed with the information already in the order of your outline.

11. Do not write the same information down twice when you find it in another source.

12. Don't spend too much time reading without getting any notes completed. Keep up with deadlines for completing notes.

WORKING WITH SINGULAR AND PLURAL FORM

Rewrite each sentence. Correct the errors by changing singular nouns, pronouns, and verbs to the plural form. Also find and correct errors in capitalization, punctuation, and use of apostrophes.

1. It chases its prey, then when they get it they eat it.

2. He can stay under water for a long time, but they have to come up for air.

3. The bear hibernates and they eat a lot in the summer.

4. The polar bear has non-skid feet which allows them to move with great speed.

5. Some food Whales eat are: small crustaceans, cuttlefish.

6. Koala's drink its mothers milk inside the pouch they are carried in.

7. An Elephants cheek are often 12 inches long and weigh 7 to 8 pound's each.

WORKING WITH SINGULAR AND PLURAL FORM (continued)

8. Arctic foxes thick white fur makes it almost invisible.

9. Animals gets its food by going out at night and hunting for their food.

10. If an animal is coming, He will lay down and stay very still until he is gone.

11. They are a very beautiful and interesting animal.

12. An Opossums ears are thin black they have no hair on their ears.

13. Koala's are three feet long and weigh 25 pounds when it reaches maturity.

14. The tigers has a very unique way of hunting.

15. Rabbits are vegetarians he enjoys eating lettuce and leaves.

REPORT WRITING:
*   HINTS FOR STUDENTS*

USE PLURAL FORM

Write your report in the plural. You are telling about all animals of the kind you have chosen, not just one. Use "<u>They-them-their</u>." Be sure that your verbs are plural to match your subjects. Not "Rabbits is." "Rabbits are" would be correct. You should say, "Koalas can only eat leaves. They live in eucalyptus trees. They also get water from these leaves."

WATCH PLURALS AND POSSESSIVES

<u>Examples</u>:   Foxes eat meat. (Plural)
A tiger's tail is striped. (Possessive)
Tigers are carnivorous animals. (Plural)
A bat's sight is very poor. (Possessive)

DO NOT USE APOSTROPHES WHEN YOUR MEANING IS MORE THAN ONE. WE USE APOSTROPHES TO SHOW POSSESSION--SOMETHING BELONGING TO THE ANIMAL.

An exception to the above rule is the word <u>its</u>. <u>It's</u> is a contraction, meaning, "It is." <u>Its</u> without the apostrophe is the possessive form of this word.

<u>Example</u>: The animal eats <u>its</u> meat raw. <u>It's</u> the meanest animal.

WATCH "THEIR", "THERE", AND "THEY'RE"

<u>Their</u> is the possessive form, such as: "The cat followed the mice to <u>their</u> home." This means the home belongs to the mice.
<u>There</u> means a place, such as: "We went over <u>there</u>," or "<u>There</u> is the house we want to see."
<u>They're</u> is the contraction form, meaning, "They are," such as: "<u>They're</u> running very quickly."

THERE IS NO SUCH WORD AS <u>ALOT</u>. IT IS TWO WORDS! EXAMPLE: "THEY HAVE <u>A LOT</u> OF FUN!"

<u>ALSO</u>, DO NOT CAPITALIZE THE NAME OF YOUR ANIMAL IN YOUR REPORT, WHEN NOT THE FIRST WORD OF A SENTENCE.

EDITING, REVISING, AND PROOFREADING: HINTS FOR STUDENTS

POST THESE HINTS FOR STUDENTS TO REFER TO WHEN THEY ARE FINISHED WITH THEIR ROUGH DRAFTS. REMIND THEM TO READ THROUGH THESE HINTS AND ANALYZE THEIR PAPERS, ACCORDING TO THESE QUESTIONS AND SUGGESTIONS.

1. Read your paper to someone else, or have someone else read it, to see if they understand what you have written.

2. Put your paper away for a while, if you have time. It helps to come back to it a little later and reread it.

3. Is the meaning of each sentence clear? Do you need to add more details to make it more clear to someone else, what you are trying to say?

4. Is each sentence a complete thought? Did you use any sentence fragments?

5. Did you use any "run-on" sentences? Did you stop and use punctuation at the end of each thought, instead of using too many "ands" between thoughts?

6. Did you leave out little words or confuse little words that are similar to each other?

7. Are you happy with the order of the sentences and/or paragraphs in your paper?

8. Did you capitalize names, and words at the beginning of sentences?

9. Did you check your spelling? A good way to do this is to underline every word in your paper that you are sure is correct, then look up any word that you have not underlined.

10. Did you use the correct punctuation at the end of each sentence? Did you check for places where you may have needed to use question marks?

HOW TO FINISH YOUR ANIMAL RESEARCH REPORT

ROUGH DRAFT

The first copy of your report will be considered as a rough draft. It will need to be proofread and edited carefully before you make your final copy. Please ask two different people to read your rough draft, to help with suggestions for revising and editing, and to check your proofreading.

FINAL COPY

Copy your report carefully, in your best penmanship. Use ink or type your report, if possible.

BIBLIOGRAPHY

Make a list of the books you have used for your research. List any book you took notes from and others you spent much time reading through, looking for information. List your books in alphabetical order according to the author's last name. Include page numbers, or state "Whole book" or "Most of book", etc.

Examples:

August, John. Whales are Mammals, pp. 67,70-75.

Caradine, Ben. The Strangest Creatures on Earth, p. 89.

Smith, Josephine. The Ferocious Cats, Whole book.

COVER

Design a cover with the name of your animal and your name. This may include a copied or self-drawn picture of your animal. You will be required to include one self-drawn picture in your report somewhere.

SECTION FIVE

PLANT UNIT

MATERIALS FOR ALL STUDENTS

PLANT INFORMATION CHART

ORGANIZATION LESSON: FOLLOWING AN OUTLINE

NOTE TAKING PRACTICE 1-2--UNDERLINING KEY WORDS

NOTE TAKING PRACTICE 3-4--WRITING KEY WORDS

NOTE TAKING PRACTICE 5-6
WRITING NOTES UNDER CORRECT HEADINGS

NOTE TAKING PRACTICE 7-8
CHANGING NOTES TO SENTENCE FORM

WEB RESEARCH LESSON:
ORGANIZATION USING THE MINDMAPPING APPROACH

RESEARCH REPORT IDEAS

INQUIRIES: EXPERIMENTS AND OBSERVATIONS

INQUIRIES: RESEARCH AND INVESTIGATIONS

PLANT INFORMATION CHART

The following chart will help you to organize information as you complete assignments on plants. Each of the categories used in outlines throughout the plant unit is explained.

Plant Classification--group, family, type of plant

A. Plant Group
   Thallophytes
   Bryophytes
   Pteridophytes
   Spermatophytes--angiosperms
   Spermatophytes--gymnosperms

B. Type of Plant
   (Thallophytes)--algae, fungi, lichens
   (Bryophytes)--mosses, liverworts
   (Pteridophytes)--ferns, horsetails, club mosses
   (Spermatophytes--angiosperms)--true flowering plants with
       seeds--garden flowers, deciduous trees and bushes,
       grasses
   (Spermatophytes--gymnosperms)--mostly evergreens with
       needles and scales, with seeds usually contained in cones

Structure or Parts of Plants--description and functions of plants and parts of plants

A. Roots
B. Stems
C. Leaves
D. Flowers
E. Seeds
F. Fruits
G. Cones
H. Other

Plant Information Chart (continued)

Plant Habitats--where plants live, types of plant communities

A. World Regions--polar, temperate, tropical, subtropical climates
B. Continents
C. Countries
D. Plant Communities
  Forest--coniferous, deciduous, rain, tropical rain, etc.
  Grassland--prairies, savannas, steppes, pampas, plains,
    pastures, etc.
  Desert--very dry regions
  Tundra--cold, treeless regions
  Aquatic regions--oceans, seas, lakes, streams, ponds, wetlands,
    seashores, bogs, marshes, etc.

Life and Growth of Plants--factors affecting life and growth

A. Life cycles and reproduction--pollination, fertilization
B. Water and moisture
C. Light
D. Soil conditions--minerals
E. Food Production--photosynthesis, parasitic relationships
F. Temperature
G. Other

90

ORGANIZATION LESSON: FOLLOWING AN OUTLINE

ORGANIZATION OUTLINE

I. DESCRIPTION
   A. FAMILY GROUP
   B. ROOTS
   C. STEMS
   D. LEAVES
   E. FLOWERS
   F. SEEDS
   G. CONES

II. HABITAT
   A. WORLD REGIONS
   B. FORESTS
   C. GRASSLANDS
   D. DESERTS
   E. TUNDRA
   F. WATER REGIONS

III. LIFE AND GROWTH
   A. REPRODUCTION
   B. WATER
   C. LIGHT
   D. SOIL CONDITIONS
   E. FOOD PRODUCTION
   F. TEMPERATURE

ORGANIZATION LESSON

Read each of the following statements. Decide where it would fit on the outline. Label each statement according to the Roman Numeral and the letter it would fit under. When you are finished labeling, cut apart the statements and sort them into the three main groups: Description, Habitat, or Life and Growth. Then organize the statements in each group in a logical order, following the subtopics. Glue or staple the statements down to a piece of paper in the order that you have chosen, as if you were going to write three paragraphs, one about each group, using the given statements.

Example: _III-E_ Plants can store the food they produce for later use.

_____1. Some leaves are simple leaves, some are compound.

_____2. Seeds are spread by wind and insects, then grow into new plants.

_____3. Plants cover most of the earth, but do not grow in areas that are always covered by ice.

_____4. Plants cannot survive very long under icy conditions.

_____5. Some plants only produce one flower, while others produce many.

_____6. Plants in extremely dry areas grow a long way apart.

_____7. Grains of pollen are sometimes carried by the wind from one plant to another.

_____8. Plants produce their own food through photosynthesis.

_____9. Root systems are either taproot or fibrous.

_____10. Spruce trees are an example from the conifer family group.

_____11. Seedlings, small shrubs, and wild flowers often grow under the trees in wooded areas.

_____12. Some cones are long and thin, while others are short and round.

_____13. Petals are usually the most colorful part of a flowering plant.

Organization Lesson (continued)

_____14. Water carries important minerals from one part of a plant to another.

_____15. Many stems are pretty and green, but some look dry and are brown.

_____16. Some dry areas have almost no plants growing at all.

_____17. Plants cannot survive without sunlight.

_____18. Tall grasses grow on most prairies.

_____19. Plants need to grow in soil that contains lots of minerals.

_____20. Conifers belong to a group called Gymnosperms.

_____21. Plants that can store water often live in very dry areas.

_____22. Some plants have to be pollinated by other plants in order to reproduce.

_____23. Fibrous roots have many tiny roots spreading out in all directions.

_____24. Most stems stand up straight and hold a plant upright.

_____25. Some plants can survive living in somewhat icy regions near the Arctic, if it is not icy the entire year round.

_____26. Cold, treeless regions, called tundra, are sometimes found at the base of mountains.

_____27. Simple and compound leaves may have toothlike, wavy, or very smooth edges.

_____28. Forests often grow in mountainous regions.

_____29. Plants without enough light will not stay green.

_____30. Good soil contains minerals that plants need for growth.

_____31. Cones come in many different shapes and sizes.

_____32. Grasslands usually cover land that is very flat.

NOTE TAKING PRACTICE 1

Underline the key words in the following statements:

1. Seeds contain stored up food to be used for growth.

2. As seeds grow, roots develop which seek out water and minerals.

3. Tiny root hairs grow into the soil and absorb water and minerals.

4. Plants get food from the air when they take in carbon dioxide.

5. Plants make starch and sugar from carbon and other elements.

6. All plants grow either from seeds or buds.

7. Sepals are green leaves around a bud which protect it as it grows.

8. Plants will produce food for themselves as long as they live.

9. Plants provide nourishment for the animals that we eat.

10. Roots of water plants might be floating on top of the water.

11. Mosses are nonflowering green plants that live on rocks and trees.

12. Thallophytes are fungi, bacteria, algae, and lichens.

13. Club mosses are small evergreen seedless plants, not true mosses.

14. Deciduous trees lose their leaves every autumn.

15. Seeds cannot grow without warmth, moisture, oxygen, and light.

16. The surroundings in which plants live are called their habitats.

17. Groups of plants living in the same habitat are called communities.

18. Ferns live in temperate climates.

19. Liverworts and mosses grow in moist, shady places.

20. Plants are found in oceans, lakes, rivers, and ponds.

NOTE TAKING PRACTICE 2

Underline the key words in the following statements:

1. Most roots grow underground, but some grow on top of the ground.

2. Stems are useful for supporting leaves and flowers as they grow.

3. Buds may grow in several different places on a stem.

4. Points where leaves join stems are called nodes.

5. Buds may become flowers, leaves, or even new branches.

6. Some plants live completely underwater, but near the surface.

7. Trees in tropical forests grow very close together.

8. Small seedlings and flowers may grow on the ground under trees.

9. Some plants are able to live under extreme conditions.

10. Plants need sunlight, precipitation, and rich soil to grow well.

11. Most plants have roots to absorb water and minerals.

12. Plants are living organisms that produce their own food.

13. Carrots, parsnips, and beets have large taproots that store food.

14. Most plants are pollinated due to wind or insects.

15. Wind pollinated flowers are usually small and clustered.

16. Insect pollinated flowers have bright colors and strong scents.

17. Most desert plants have long, deep roots that can search for water.

18. Some plants are parasites and live on other plants to obtain food.

19. Plants cannot move about under their own power like animals can.

20. The ages of trees may be determined by counting their annual rings.

NOTE TAKING PRACTICE 3

Write the key words from the following in note form:

1. Plants may be affected by other plants growing in the same area.

_____

2. Chaparrals are covered with thick growths of shrubs and trees.

_____

3. Hemlocks, Douglas-firs, and cedars grow in coniferous forests.

_____

4. Vines climb high on trees in most rain forests.

_____

5. Chlorophyll in leaves absorbs sunlight during photosynthesis.

_____

6. The majority of plants have leaves that are broad and flat.

_____

7. Networks of veins carry water throughout leaves.

_____

8. Some flowers are really a series of tiny flowers that look like one.

_____

9. Flowers contain the reproductive parts of flowering plants.

_____

10. All cone-bearing plants have uncovered seeds.

_____

NOTE TAKING PRACTICE 4

Write the key words from the following in note form:

1. All flowering plants have enclosed seeds.

   _____

2. The sprouting of seeds is called germination.

   _____

3. Water escapes from leaves of a plant and goes back into the air.

   _____

4. The largest plants are the conifers, some as high as 300 feet.

   _____

5. Ferns and horsetails are primitive plants that reproduce by spores.

   _____

6. Lichens grow very slowly and live for a long period of time.

   _____

7. Plants living in dark places need large leaves to catch light.

   _____

8. Plants living in the open need small, strong leaves due to wind.

   _____

9. Plants living in water have feathery leaves water passes through.

   _____

10. Leaves that contain many leaflets are called compound leaves.

    _____

NOTE TAKING PRACTICE 5

**Put the following information under the correct heading, in note form:**

Description

Habitat

Plant Life and Growth

1. Conifers are trees or shrubs with narrow, needle-like or scale-like leaves.
2. Any group of plants living in the same place is called a plant community.
3. Plants produce their own food and store it for use as it is needed for growth.
4. Forests of trees need plenty of rainfall in order to grow.
5. Simple leaves have only one blade, while compound leaves have two or more blades.
6. Tropical evergreen forests exist in hot, wet areas.
7. Many land plants cannot survive in icy regions.
8. The most colorful parts of flowers are their petals.
9. Roots grow downward into the soil.
10. Seeds receive moisture from the ground to help them grow.

NOTE TAKING PRACTICE 6

Put the following information under the correct heading, in note form:

Description

Habitat

Plant Life and Growth

1. Some plants have smooth green stems, while others have stems that are rough and brown.
2. Roots of plants may be fibrous, with many small roots spreading out in many directions.
3. Stems grow upward into the air and support the plant.
4. Grasses cannot live in dry areas such as deserts.
5. Some plants only live for a few weeks while others live thousands of years.
6. Leaves may have toothy, wavy, or smooth edges.
7. Climate is the main factor determining where plants can live.
8. Annual growth layers on a tree are called rings.
9. Only ferns can live on the floor of a tropical forest.
10. Plants called perennials live for many years.

NOTE TAKING PRACTICE 7

Change the following notes to sentence form:

HOW SEEDS ARE SPREAD

Some plants-exploding seed pods-fling seeds-air

_____

Some plants-flying seeds-carried far-wind

_____

Some flying seeds-land in water-carried away-currents

_____

Small, light seeds-scattered-wind-carried distances

_____

Some fruits-own parachutes-float-wind

_____

Wind-shakes heads of plants-seeds fall

_____

Some plants-spread own seeds-seed cases burst- as dried by sun

_____

Some seeds-small hooks, burs-stick to fur of animals-spread

_____

NOTE TAKING PRACTICE 8

Change the following notes to sentence form:

HOW FLOWERS ARE POLLINATED

Butterflies-pollinate flowers-feed on nectar

_____

Bees-like nectar-in back of flowers-climb inside-pick up pollen-carry

_____

Insects-carry pollen-one flower, another flower

_____

Pollen scattered-wind, water, insects

_____

Pollen grains from anther-carried to stigma-next flower

_____

Butterflies attracted-sweet scents-flowers

_____

Some flowers-rely on birds-attracted-bright colors-sweet nectar

_____

Some flowers pollinated-bats, mice, possums, slugs-carry pollen

_____

101

WEB RESEARCH LESSON: ORGANIZATION USING THE MINDMAPPING APPROACH

READ AND ANALYZE EACH STATEMENT. CREATE A MINDMAP BY TRANSFERRING THE INFORMATION TO THE CORRECT BRANCH OF THE WEB.

KINDS OF PLANTS

1. Plants of this type do not form embryos.

2. This family includes mosses and their relatives.

3. Most of the plants in this group reproduce through cones.

4. These plants are called the "true" flowering plants.

5. Reproduction of these plants is by means of a flower which contains the pollen in the stamen and the egg in the pistil.

6. Many of these plants reproduce through spores.

7. Horsetails and club mosses belong in this category.

8. These plants do not have true roots, stems, or leaves.

9. Pines, spruces, firs, cedars, and redwoods belong to this group.

10. Most members of this group are evergreens with needles or scalelike leaves.

11. Liverworts and mosses grow in moist, shady places.

12. Algae and fungi are plants belonging to this plant kingdom.

13. Ferns usually have well developed, large compound leaves.

14. Every seed in this plant group contains an embryo, or a miniature flowering plant.

15. Hornworts belong to the same family as mosses and liverworts.

102

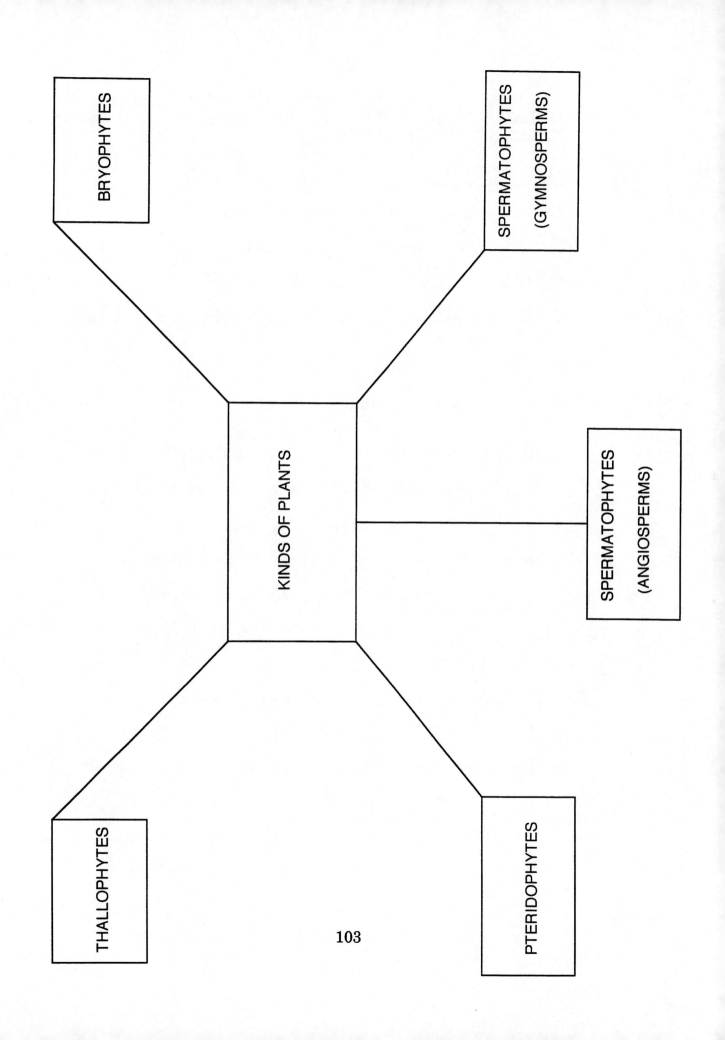

103

READ AND ANALYZE EACH STATEMENT. CREATE A MINDMAP BY TRANSFERRING THE INFORMATION TO THE CORRECT BRANCH OF THE WEB.

PARTS OF PLANTS

1. Seeds come in many different shapes and sizes.

2. The function of flowers is to produce seeds.

3. Stems support plants while they grow.

4. The size of seeds is not related to the size of plants which will grow from them.

5. Roots of some water plants float freely in water.

6. Most flowers consist of the calyx, the corolla, the stamens, and the pistils.

7. Stems may be rough and brown, or green and smooth.

8. Some leaves are long and slender, while some are rounded.

9. Most plants have leaves which are broad and flat.

10. There are two types of enclosed seeds, monocots and dicots.

11. Fibrous roots have many slender roots fanning out in all directions.

12. Taproots have one root longer than the others, and the roots grow straight down.

13. The trunk and branches of trees are actually stems.

14. The corolla is all the petals of a flower.

15. Most leaves are arranged in definite patterns.

104

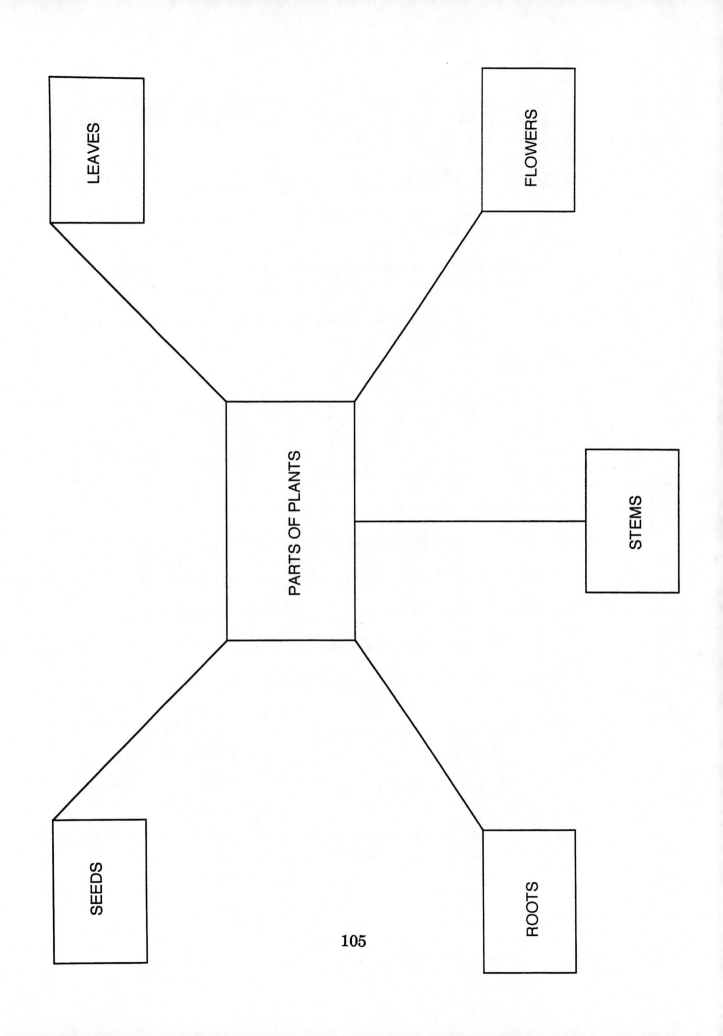

105

READ AND ANALYZE EACH STATEMENT. CREATE A MINDMAP BY TRANSFERRING THE INFORMATION TO THE CORRECT BRANCH OF THE WEB.

HABITATS OF PLANTS

1. Trees grow so close together in tropical forests that little sunlight reaches the ground.

2. Plants that live in water often have air spaces in their stems and leaves.

3. Plants that live in cold, treeless areas must survive snowy, icy conditions.

4. Cactus plants live only in very dry places.

5. Roots of plants in dry areas are long and reach deep into the ground.

6. Low growing plants, such as mosses, shrubs, and wildflowers can grow in cold, treeless regions.

7. Some plants live completely underwater.

8. Many open, flat areas have only grass growing, with no trees.

9. Grassy areas with widely spaced trees are called savannas.

10. Many different kinds of plants grow in forests, not just trees.

11. In a deciduous forest, trees drop their leaves in cold seasons.

12. Most water plants live near the surface, or in shallow water, so they can receive sunlight.

13. Conifers may appear at the base of a high mountain tundra.

14. Plants in extremely dry regions grow a long way apart.

15. Only short grasses grow in the grasslands called steppes.

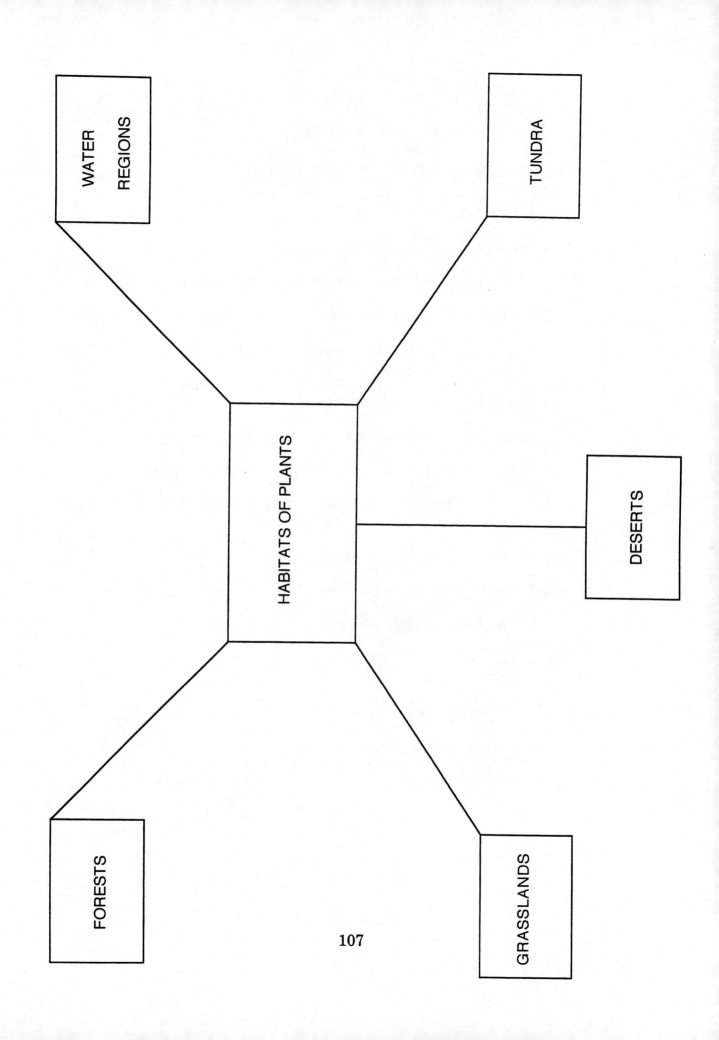

WATER REGIONS

TUNDRA

HABITATS OF PLANTS

DESERTS

FORESTS

GRASSLANDS

READ AND ANALYZE EACH STATEMENT. CREATE A MINDMAP BY TRANSFERRING THE INFORMATION TO THE CORRECT BRANCH OF THE WEB.

LIFE AND GROWTH OF PLANTS

1. Plants need sunlight in order to grow well.

2. Seeds store food for future growth.

3. Flowers contain the reproductive parts of most flowering plants.

4. Plants are affected by heat and cold while they grow.

5. Moisture travels through the roots and up stems to the rest of the plant.

6. Plants grow naturally toward light.

7. Seeds need a proper temperature in order to sprout.

8. Many flowering plants are pollinated by bees and other insects.

9. One of the most important factors affecting growth of plants is the amount of warmth or cold they receive.

10. Plants need water in order to survive.

11. Water escapes into the air from the surface of leaves.

12. Ferns can grow with less light than most plants.

13. Some plants regenerate themselves from cuttings off a larger plant.

14. Food enters plants through root hairs.

15. Leaves make starch and sugar, as food for themselves, from carbon and other elements.

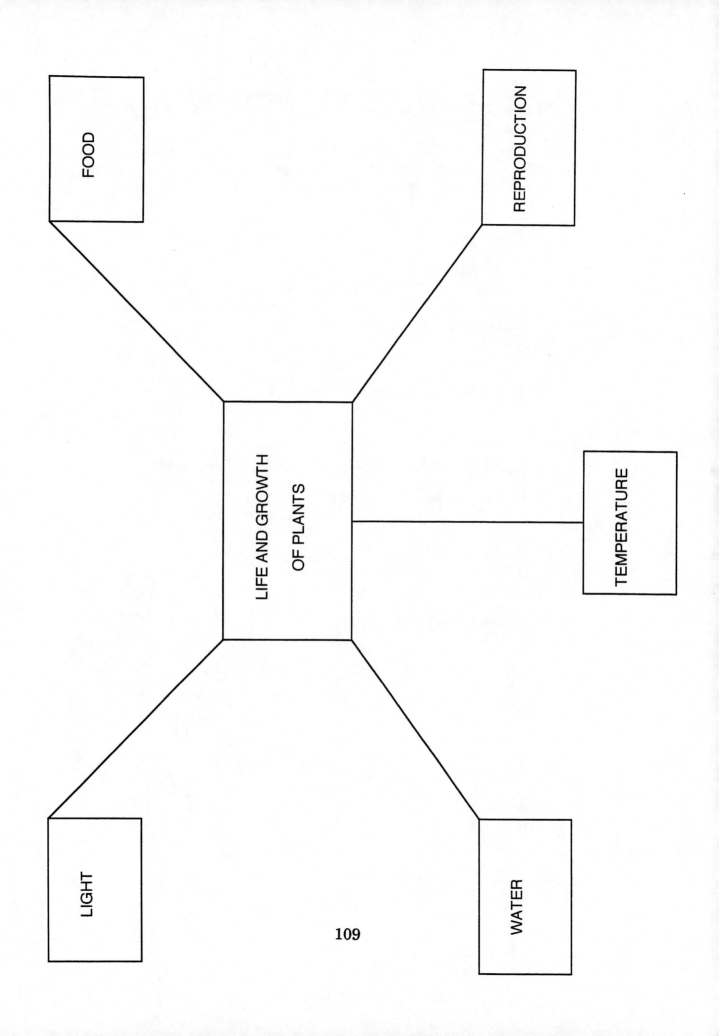

FOOD

REPRODUCTION

LIFE AND GROWTH
OF PLANTS

TEMPERATURE

LIGHT

WATER

109

RESEARCH REPORT IDEAS

Use one of these ideas to design your own research report. Create an outline and fill out note cards. Follow the rest of the report writing procedures, as directed by your teacher.

Plant Pests
aphid
apple maggot
cankerworm
gypsy moth
tent caterpillar
weevil
leafhopper
cutworm
Mediterranean fruit fly

Plant Products
alcohol
cork
perfume
lumber
paper
rubber
turpentine
tar
dye

Plant Diseases
blight
fungal disease
mildew
rust
wilt
rot

Important People
George Washington Carver
Luther Burbank
Gregor Mendel
Charles Darwin
Carolus Linnaeus

Important Plant Crops
alfalfa
barley
peanut
sugar beet
cotton
rice
potato
soybean
wheat
tobacco
sugar cane
oats

INQUIRIES: EXPERIMENTS AND OBSERVATIONS

CHOOSE FROM THE FOLLOWING:

1. Soak a bean seed overnight in a refrigerator. Remove the seed coat. Illustrate the seed coat and the cotyledons, then the leaves, stems, and roots of the growing embryo.

2. Plant some soaked bean seeds. Watch them grow for several weeks and illustrate what you see as changes occur.

3. Plant seeds. Note and record the number of days before seedlings come through the soil (germination), the development of the first leaves, the appearance of flowers, and the development of fruit. Measure the height and width of the plant as it grows, at regular intervals.

4. Collect roots with different types of root systems. Examine their differences and explain the functions of different parts.

5. Look at root hairs through a microscope and record what you see.

6. Plant several plants, varying the types of soil conditions. After a period of time, examine the differences in the growth of their roots.

7. Grow several plants. Expose them to different conditions, varying light, temperature, and/or moisture. Compare and illustrate your results.

8. Obtain a potato and let it grow "eyes." Watch for buds to appear. Plant the potato and describe what happens as it grows.

9. Collect twigs from different trees. Compare them and identify their differences.

111

Inquiries: Experiments and Observations (continued)

10. Look for terminal bud scars on twigs from different trees. Notice the amount of the year's growth for each one, by measuring the distance between bud scars. Discuss the likenesses and differences. (One year's growth is the amount between bud scars.)

11. Measure the distances between internodes on the same stem. Explain the results of your measurements.

12. Examine different types of simple leaves. Illustrate them and explain their different characteristics, such as edges and vein patterns.

13. Find examples of leaves with different leaf arrangements and create a poster with them. Label the different leaves with the names of their leaf arrangement patterns.

14. Illustrate what you see when you look at a root tip through a microscope.

15. Experiment with plants that you keep in a light place. Keep track of their growth, looking for proof of their bending toward light. Turn one of them around each day and leave the other one alone. Explain the differences in the growth of the two plants.

16. Experiment with the growth of plants, with and without soil, water, and/or air. Plant seeds under the following conditions:
   A. Plant some seeds in soil and some in water. Keep the soil moist and give both groups the same amount of light.
   B. Plant seeds in soil. Keep the soil moist for one group of plants, let the soil dry out around the other.
   C. Plant seeds in two jars of soil. Put a lid on one of the jars and leave the other one open. Give both jars light, and water the soil in the open jar.
Explain the results of each experiment, indicating the necessary conditions for growth of plants.

17. Place twigs in colored water and plain water. Check the results after a day or two, then report on what happened and why.

18. Plant corn seeds sideways, upside down, and right side up. Keep all other conditions the same. After seeds have sprouted, carefully remove and compare the way stems and roots have grown. Describe your results and explain the differences.

Inquiries: Experiments and Observations (continued)

19. Plant tomato seeds with a group of classmates. When the plants are strong and healthy, take them to different homes and transplant them. Identify the conditions at each home. Measure their growth at regular intervals and chart your measurements. Compare your results with your classmates.

20. Demonstrate how different trees can be identified by making a collection of leaves, bark, flowers, and seeds from different trees. Study them and label them according to the trees they are from.

21. Select a special tree to study. Illustrate it and label the three main parts. Watch for changes in each part, over a period of time. Illustrate and explain these changes.

22. Distinguish between coniferous and deciduous trees. List names of trees in each group.

23. Categorize the different types of leaves by making leaf collections and identifying the different kinds.

24. Make leaf prints and distinguish between simple and compound leaves as you examine leaf patterns, vein patterns and edges.

25. Make bark collections. Study the different types and identify the trees from which they have been collected.

26. Examine trees that have been damaged by fire or insects. Compare them to undamaged trees of the same kinds.

27. Construct a terrarium with mosses, ferns, and a few small animals. Explain the dependence plants and animals have on each other in order to survive.

Inquiries: Experiments and Observations (continued)

28. Experiment with two plants, placing one in light and one in dark. Report on the comparisons and contrasts in your results.

29. Select a tree on the playground to study. Chart the conditions it faces each day, such as snow, rain, sun, appearance of birds and/or insects on it, indications of plant diseases, etc. Discuss and illustrate the changes that you see over a period of time, due to these conditions.

30. Identify the trees and bushes on your school grounds. Illustrate them and label their parts.

31. Plant several different types of seeds (grass, corn, bean, radish, etc.) in the same container of soil. Water them and keep them warm. Compare the differences in their growth as you watch for: when the seeds break through the soil, when the first true leaves appear on the seedlings, how tall they grow, etc. Present your results to others.

32. Collect and label seeds from different plants. Plant some of them and compare the size of the seedlings to the size of the seeds they came from. Continue this comparison as the plants grow.

33. Build a terrarium with mosses, ferns, and other aquatic plants. Observe and illustrate the changes in the plants over time.

34. Place several types of seeds between wet paper towels. Keep moist. Observe changes and compare the different plants as the seeds sprout and begin to grow.

35. Place seeds of the same type between wet paper towels. Try different conditions. Put some of them in a dark place but keep moist. Put some of them in a light place but don't give them any more water. Put some of them in a very warm place, and some of them in a very cold place. Give some of them light, water, and warmth. Observe growth and determine which conditions are the most important for optimum growth.

36. Obtain cross sections of several tree trunks. Determine the ages of the trees they came from. Compare thickness of the sections to their ages. Explain why some of the sections are thicker than others at the same age or even at younger ages.

37. Grow molds on old bread or rotten fruit. Examine them under a microscope. Illustrate and label the parts that you see.

Inquiries: Experiments and Observations (continued)

38. Crush a spore case from a moss plant and examine it under a
microscope. Identify the number of spores that are contained in
one spore case.

39. Illustrate the tiny moss plants that you see through a microscope.

40. Experiment to see if plants use the color from light to help them
grow. Plant seeds in four different boxes. Cover each box with
colored cellophane of a different color. Place in sunlight.
Observe and report any differences you may see in the growth of
the plants.

41. Observe slides showing cells of different parts of plants. Illustrate
what you see and label the parts of the cells.

42. Place a complete stalk of celery in water containing food coloring.
Leave it for a day, then examine the stalk and the leaves.
Explain how this is related to water movement in plants.

43. Observe a dandelion flower through a magnifying glass. Draw
what you see. Tell why you believe dandelions are able to
reproduce so easily and quickly. Read about dandelions to find
out if you are correct.

44. Experiment with a small houseplant. Coat the underside of
several leaves and the topside of several different leaves with
petroleum jelly. Watch the leaves for several days and explain
what happens to some of the leaves and why.

45. Obtain a leaf with its stem. Put the stem through a small hole in a
piece of cardboard. Seal around the hole with clay. Put the
cardboard on top of a jar filled with water, with the stem in the
water and the leaf above the cardboard. Invert a second jar over
the leaf part of the plant. Put the jars in a light, warm place
and leave them for a day. Summarize what you did, and explain
the process you see happening in the upper jar.

INQUIRIES: RESEARCH AND INVESTIGATIONS

CHOOSE FROM THE FOLLOWING:

1. Discuss the function of roots, stems, leaves, and flowers in a plant.

2. Draw a picture of a stem. Label the nodes, internodes, and buds.

3. Prepare crayon rubbings of leaves showing their stems and leaflets, in detail.

4. Explain how flowers use food to get energy to produce seeds.

5. Describe the plant processes of photosynthesis, transpiration, and respiration.

6. Draw a flower and label its parts.

7. Explain why green plants can make their own food.

8. Report on plant parasites and how they get their food.

9. Illustrate a tree and label the three main parts. Explain why each part is important to the growth and survival of the tree.

10. Distinguish between coniferous and deciduous trees. List the well known trees in each group.

11. Prepare a report on forests, forestry, and the lumber industry.

12. Research why trees are important for soil conservation, helping to prevent floods, and as windbreaks.

Inquiries: Research and Investigations (continued)

13. Discover unusual trees such as the Banyan, the Baobab, and the Eucalyptus. Illustrate them and explain why they are called unusual.

14. Outline the animal-plant life cycle. Prepare a chart or poster for your classroom bulletin board.

15. Name the plants that have edible roots. Prepare some of these roots for you and your classmates to taste.

16. Categorize the food we get from leaves, stems, fruits, seeds, and flowers of plants.

17. Explain the life cycle of a lichen.

18. Research poisonous plants and explain why each one is dangerous to humans or other animals.

19. Compile a list of living things that have the characteristics of both plants and animals.

20. Compile a list of plants that survive by capturing insects for food, and explain why they need to do this. Illustrate these plants, showing the different ways they capture their food.

21. List plants that cannot make their own food and explain how they go about getting food.

22. Explain which plants reproduce through spores. Explain the process.

23. Design a study of the importance of farm plants in your area and explain the conditions under which they grow.

24. Prepare posters showing specific plants or plant families.

25. Design a poster showing the stages in the life of a particular plant.

26. Explain the importance of flowering plants to humans.

27. Discuss the part flowers play in the survival of a flowering plant.

28. Research plants with underground stems. Explain the difference between these stems and stems that grow above the ground.

Inquiries: Research and Investigations (continued)

29. Explain how a leaf changes light energy into chemical energy.

30. Interpret the role of insects in helping flowers to reproduce themselves.

31. Discuss the role of birds as a necessary part of the lives of some flowering plants.

32. Prepare a chart of the five plant groups, showing plants belonging to each group.

33. Explain how fungi get their food.

34. Explain how plants of the thallophyte group reproduce.

35. Report on the spermatophyte plant group, explaining the differences between angiosperms and gymnosperms.

36. Research how ferns are related to the formation of coal.

37. Explain geotropism and the effect it has on root growth and plant growth.

38. Categorize annuals, biennials, and perennials according to their differences.

39. Interpret the effect temperature has on whether plants are annuals, biennials, or perennials.

40. Demonstrate how a flower protects a seed as it grows.

Inquiries: Research and Investigations (continued)

41. Report on the growth of bacteria, both good and bad.

42. Explain why pteridophytes were among the earliest plants on earth.

43. Identify the importance of sepals in a flowering plant.

44. Discuss the different scents flowers have, in order to attract birds, butterflies, and other insects to help with pollination.

45. Outline the steps showing how most trees and grasses are pollinated.

46. Research the yucca plant and discover the unique way it is pollinated.

47. Illustrate the habitats for different plants, showing the other plants that share the same community.

48. List the plants that belong in each habitat, and outline the conditions that allow them to survive there.

49. Name the plants that are succulents. Explain how they are different from other plants.

50. List examples of the major food plants grown in the area where you live. Relate where they are shipped to, around the country or around the world.

SECTION SIX

PLANT UNIT

GREEN STRAND MATERIALS

PLANT OUTLINE (FOR ALL PLANTS)--GREEN

SPECIFIC PLANT LIST--GREEN

SPECIFIC PLANT OUTLINE--GREEN

PLANT OUTLINE
Green

Use the following outline. Find as much information as possible about <u>all</u> plants. Look for something about each topic in the outline. Use a separate note card for each topic.

I. Differences Between Plants and Animals
(food, air, movement, feeling, growth, other)

II. Kinds of Plants
(family, group, types of plants)

III. Parts of Plants
(roots, stems, leaves, flowers, seeds, fruits, cones, other)

IV. Habitats of Plants
(world regions, continents, countries, plant communities)

V. Life and Growth of Plants
(life cycles, reproduction, water, light, soil conditions, food production, temperature, other)

SPECIFIC PLANT LIST
Green

Please choose plants from this list for your <u>specific</u> plant report. They will be easier to find information on than some of the other plants you might choose, because they are more common.

WELL KNOWN FLOWERS (GARDEN)

aster	bleeding heart	chrysanthemum
crocus	daffodil	nasturtium
pansy	snapdragon	fuchsia
geranium	marigold	iris
dahlia	petunia	forget-me-not
poppy	primrose	lily
pink	tulip	rose

WELL KNOWN FLOWERS (WILD)

buttercup	goldenrod	columbine
touch-me-not	trillium	fireweed
Oregon grape	dandelion	violet
black-eyed Susan	daisy	

HERBS

basil	catnip	mint
peppermint	sage	parsley
thyme	rosemary	spearmint
licorice	caraway	

SHRUBS

azalea	hydrangea	pussy willow
lilac	rhododendron	forsythia

TREES

pine	spruce	fir
maple	birch	elm
oak	magnolia	ash
cottonwood	willow	redwood
dogwood	sequoia	palm
cedar	hemlock	alder

SPECIFIC PLANT OUTLINE
Green

Use the following outline. Find as much information as possible about the <u>specific</u> plant you choose. Look for something about each of the topics in the outline. Use a separate note card for each topic.

I. CLASSIFICATION

Plant group and type of plant

II. STRUCTURE OR PARTS OF PLANT

Roots, stems, leaves, flowers, seeds, fruits, cones, other

III. PLANT HABITAT

World regions, continents, countries, plant communities

IV. LIFE AND GROWTH

Life cycle, reproduction, water, light, soil conditions,
food production, temperature, other

SECTION SEVEN

PLANT UNIT

BLUE STRAND MATERIALS

PLANT OUTLINE (FOR ALL PLANTS)--BLUE

SPECIFIC PLANT LIST--BLUE

SPECIFIC PLANT OUTLINE--BLUE

PLANT OUTLINE
Blue

Use the following outline. Find as much information as possible about all plants. Look for something about each topic and subtopic in the outline. Use a separate note card for each subtopic.

I. Differences Between Plants and Animals
    A. Food
    B. Air
    C. Movement and Feeling
    D. Growth

II. Kinds of Plants
    A. Thallophytes
    B. Bryophytes
    C. Pteridophytes
    D. Spermatophytes (angiosperms)
    E. Spermatophytes (gymnosperms)

III. Parts of Plants
    A. Roots
    B. Stems
    C. Leaves
    D. Flowers
    E. Seeds
    F. Fruits
    G. Cones
    H. Other

IV. Habitats of Plants
    A. World Regions
    B. Continents
    C. Countries
    D. Plant Communities

V. Life and Growth of Plants
    A. Life cycles and reproduction
    B. Water
    C. Light
    D. Soil conditions
    E. Food production
    F. Temperature
    G. Other

SPECIFIC PLANT LIST
Blue

Please choose plants from this list for your <u>specific</u> plant report. They will be easier to find information on than some of the other plants you might choose, because they are more common.

WELL KNOWN FLOWERS (GARDEN)

aster	bleeding heart	chrysanthemum
morning glory	lily	sweet alyssum
crocus	daffodil	nasturtium
babies'-breath	pansy	snapdragon
fuchsia	geranium	marigold
bachelor's-button	iris	primrose
dahlia	petunia	forget-me-not
poppy	sunflower	tiger lily
gladiolus	hollyhock	impatiens
pink	tulip	rose

WELL KNOWN FLOWERS (WILD)

buttercup	goldenrod	columbine
bellflower	bloodroot	bluebonnet
touch-me-not	trillium	fireweed
cockscomb	Oregon grape	dandelion
violet	gentian	hepatica
black-eyed Susan	daisy	lupine

HERBS

basil	catnip	mint
cumin	bitters	peppermint
sage	parsley	quinoa
vanilla	thyme	rosemary
spearmint	licorice	caraway

SHRUBS

azalea	hydrangea	pussy willow
acanthus	beach plum	bougainvillea
broom	forsythia	cassava
lilac	snowball	rhododendron

Specific Plant List--Blue (continued)

TREES

pine	spruce	fir
cypress	acacia	aspen
maple	birch	elm
tulip tree	tamarack	larch
oak	magnolia	beech
cottonwood	willow	redwood
dogwood	sequoia	palm
sweetgum	mahogany	hawthorn
juniper	cedar	hemlock
hickory	ash	alder

VEGETABLES

beet	corn	pea
green bean	Lima bean	cauliflower
broccoli	turnip	parsnip
Brussels sprouts	zucchini	carrot

SPECIFIC PLANT OUTLINE
Blue

Use the following outline. Find as much information as possible about the <u>specific</u> plant you choose. Look for something about each of the topics and subtopics in the outline. Use a separate note card for each subtopic.

I. CLASSIFICATION
    A. PLANT GROUP
    B. TYPE OF PLANT

II. STRUCTURE OR PARTS OF PLANT
    A. ROOTS
    B. STEMS
    C. LEAVES
    D. FLOWERS
    E. SEEDS
    F. FRUITS
    G. CONES
    H. OTHER

III. PLANT HABITAT
    A. WORLD REGION
    B. CONTINENTS
    C. COUNTRIES
    D. PLANT COMMUNITIES

IV. LIFE AND GROWTH
    A. LIFE CYCLE AND REPRODUCTION
    B. WATER AND MOISTURE
    C. LIGHT
    D. SOIL CONDITIONS
    E. FOOD PRODUCTION
    F. TEMPERATURE
    G. OTHER